Cha...
po...

by
PSYCHIC BOB

Conveyed to this plane of existence
by
Nick Pettigrew

the dailymash

Mash Books
First published in the UK in 2011 by Mash Books, an imprint of Mashed
Productions Ltd and The Daily Mash www.thedailymash.co.uk

ISBN 978-0956666215

A copy of the British Library Cataloguing in Publication Data
is available from the British Library.

Cover illlustration, design and layout:
michaelgill.eu

Printed and bound in the UK by Cox and Wyman.

Aquarius

Famous Aquatic:
DJ Jazzy Jeff

Health:
You've always been plagued with problems with your hands, mainly that you can't keep them out of your own jogging pants.

Career:
You've always been very work-orientated but this is the year when it finally dawns on you that work isn't you-orientated.

Romance:
Cynics dismiss love as nothing more than a chemical imbalance in the brain, but that only explains why you occasionally go fucking mental in Asda before passing out.

Highlight Of The Year:
Trapping your genitals in the fly of a pair of jeans, you're rushed to hospital shortly after being permanently banned from River Island

Your Lucky One-Hit Wonder:
Love Grows Where My Rosemary Goes - Edison Lighthouse

Aquarius

100 situps a day is quite impressive. Is there an equivalent exercise for your face?

Pisces

This week you'll have the difficult task of explaining to your partner why you were fired from the hospital for using the MRI scanner to see whether it was a peanut or an orange cream in your bag of Revels.

Aries

Put your hands in the air, and wave them like you just don't care. Now give me everything out of the till or I'll blow your fucking head off.

Taurus

Pinch the bridge of your nose and tilt your head back to staunch the bleeding. Oops, sorry, I haven't smacked you in the face yet, have I?

Gemini

After studying conspiracy theories at university, you decide to go for your All Hail Our Lizard Masters degree.

Cancer

Well, it's a bittersweet symphony called life. Try to make ends meet, you're a slave to money then you die. It's difficult to imagine what that's like from the depths of my 30-foot jade hot-tub hookerdrome, to be honest.

Leo

This magnificent collection
from Pronghi builds over 156
weeks into an impressive pile
of shite you'll sob at every time
you're reminded how much it
cost.

Virgo

Excellent news as your
application for Channel 5's *Are
You Britain's Fattest Herpes
Sufferer?* is accepted. Now
comes the difficult part – telling
your congregation.

Libra

Historians can be so fickle –
Lady Godiva was immortalised
for riding through Coventry
naked on a horse, but cycling
through Halfords with your
cock out didn't even make the
regional news bulletin.

Scorpio

Sitting in your solitary
confinement cell, planning
your escape, you burn with
the injustice of being jailed for
a murder you didn't commit.
Least said about all those armed
robberies you actually did
commit the better, though.

Sagittarius

After discovering from Santa
that you're not really an elf,
you journey through a magical
kingdom to New York to find
your real dad. Until you wake
up in the local park stinking of
mushrooms and piss.

Capricorn

Watching *Skins* really speaks to
you about your teenage years,
mostly that they didn't take
place in the fevered cocaine
imagination of a
Hoxton shitbag.

Aquarius

You love your girlfriend even though she has funny little habits like stealing the duvet. You do miss being able to shop in John Lewis, though.

Pisces

The moment I wake up, before I put on my makeup, I say a little prayer for you. Because when I find you, I'm going to rip your bastard arms off.

Aries

You save yourself endless painful hours in the cinema after realising that any film that uses the word 'heartwarming' on its poster is going to be marginally less fun than having arse-flavoured popcorn flicked into your eyes.

Taurus

Loneliness is a cloak you wear. And each shade of blue is always there. As well as Um Bongo stains and dried sobwank.

Gemini

You've cooked dinner, run a candlelit bath and have her favourite James Blunt CD on the stereo. Actually, you'd better throw in a bottle of champagne too. It was her best friend, after all.

Cancer

A good sense of humour has always been the most important quality in a boyfriend and your new man has the funniest 2lb cock you've ever seen.

Leo

If you take a weekend as being 5pm Friday to 9am Monday, that's 64 hours in total. D'you think that's long enough to shuffle around your flat eating toast and wondering exactly where the fuck it all went wrong?

Virgo

Then I look at you, and I know it's going to be a lovely day. Lovely day, lovely day, lovely day, lovely day. Lovely day, lovely day, lovely day, lovely day. Lovely day lov...I just ruined it, didn't I?

Libra

Your attempt at a healthy diet flounders as you try and get your five portions of fruit per day via the medium of pomegranate margaritas.

Scorpio

While your 240-linc blank verse poem entitled *Britain Is The Whore That Gave Justice AIDS* is indeed a searing indictment of modern society, it was probably the wrong choice for your CBBC presenter's audition.

Sagittarius

And please remember, this horoscope is not available in the shops. Except for the shops that sell this book. And possibly some charity shops in a few months' time.

Capricorn

Oh, hello, here's that Jason Statham chap wearing a suit and looking cross while an entire building explodes behind him. I wonder if this film's an EM Forster adaptation?

Aquarius

Your looped 'y' indicates a flamboyant personality and the forward sloping suggests impatience. But it's the fact you've written it in your own dung that's really going to banjax your parole application.

Pisces

I love rock 'n' roll, so put another dime in the jukebox baby, I love rock 'n' roll, so if you put Coldplay on I'm going to have to pull your arse out through your nose.

Aries

Home-hunting hits a rocky patch when your estate agent says that the only house in your desired area and price range is in a toy shop window.

Taurus

Be thankful that there's no such thing as the QI klaxon every time you say something idiotic in real life because your whole existence would have sounded like one long air raid warning.

Gemini

Have you ever noticed that fairly universal aspect of everyday life, eh? It's like some parallel version of the same thing that in some way highlights the ridiculousness of the original situation! Next on stage, Jack Whitehall!

Cancer

We close our eyes, we never lose a game, imagination never lets us take the blame. It's great being an England footballer.

Leo

A red-letter day for you after scientists prove that trying to create something of artistic merit requires exactly the same amount of effort and ability as going on Twitter and saying it's shit.

Virgo

An epiphany in work as you realise that you've hated being there for so long that there isn't a single piece of office furniture you haven't wiped your cock on.

Libra

You say you don't look at the mantelpiece when you're stoking the fire but that presupposes that you view vaginas as something that should have coal stuffed in them and ignited. What's fucking wrong with you?

Scorpio

To be or not to be, that is the question. What? To be, you reckon? Righto.

Sagittarius

A relationship like yours is never going to last without a lot of hard work on your part. Ideally, plenty of overtime so she has the house to herself.

Capricorn

As part of a disenfranchised minority you may feel that society is geared toward ignoring your valid world view and needs for the capitalist agenda. Shoot the living piss out of a crowded public place, that ought to convince 'em.

Aquarius

Take your first left, straight
over the roundabout, stay
in the righthand lane as it
separates, straight on for two
miles, second exit off the next
roundabout and after that I
really don't care so long as
you're the fuck away from me.

Pisces

Rooting through your parent's
attic is a real trip down memory
lane – the old board games,
the teddy bears, the wondering
if they're going to unlock the
hatch and let you out...

Aries

Why not commission a comedy
film about two stoners getting
really high and trying to find
a fast food joint? I'm not sure
potheads know quite how
funny their six-hour rambling
conversations are.

Taurus

Now, I don't want you to panic
but...actually there's absolutely
no way you're not going to
completely freak out when you
hear this. At least try and keep
away from anything sharp.

Gemini

Excitement? Adventure? A Jedi
craves not these things. But a
set of prequels with a vaguely
coherent plot and characters
that don't make your teeth throb
would be nice.

Cancer

Bored with motorway driving
you try to liven things up by
painting pictures of mohican
mutants on your windscreen and
pretending you're in *Mad Max*.

Leo

Fortunately the other mums
will never notice you've catered
your daughter's birthday party
from Iceland as you've always
been an exceptionally mediocre
cook.

Virgo

You want to say it with
diamonds for her birthday this
year but it's going to cost a
fortune to spell out "Your arse
has got huge."

Libra

No, I don't think you can
call 999 for an onset of
existential ennui. Have you
tried contacting the French
Samaritans?

Scorpio

Liven up somebody's day in
B&Q by asking the paint mixer
if they can whip up five litres in
the same shade as the dead dog
you've brought in.

Sagittarius

This week, Mercury is
ascendant, Saturn is fluxatious
and Neptune is vacillating
between effulgent and supine.
By Thursday you're going to be
absolutely knackered.

Capricorn

When god gives you lemons
you make lemonade, so I hope
you're in the mood for gallons
of messydivorceandpainfulill-
nessade.

> **"**
> *Maybe that new moisturiser is going to make you look a bit better. Yeah, the problem's always been that you're not moist enough.*
> **"**

Pisces

Famous Pisceser: Howard Jones

Health:
As a fish you are the strongest-swimming of all the star
signs, but are prone to mouth injuries whenever
somebody dangles a maggot near you.

Career:
You cannot wait to see the look on the boss's face when, after
asking what exactly you've been doing all year, you usher him into
the stationery cupboard to behold your lifesize
paperclip Velociraptor.

Romance:
Your 10th anniversary is a big occasion this year, so you've pulled
out all the stops to have a sky-writing plane spell out "I've never
been so unhappy in all my life" in smoke.

Highlight Of The Year:
Opening a multi-bag of crisps with an extra free bag and they're
the flavour you like. They'll be hearing about that down the dole
office for months to come.

Your Lucky One-Hit Wonder:
Whip It - Devo

Aquarius

GO FOR THE BURN! GIMME
20 MORE REPS! I WANNA
SEE THOSE QUADS RIPPED!
Now get changed quickly as
you've all got double maths
next.

Pisces

Will you still need me, will you
still feed me, when I'm 64? And
while we're on the subject, how
are you with catheters?

Aries

You've booked a delightful long
weekend away in a beautiful
cottage in the Lake District with
a real log fire, no phone and
stunning views of Windermere.
Perfect for your prolonged anal
scatgimp sessions.

Taurus

Remember those endless
summer holidays climbing
trees, fishing for sticklebacks
and camping under an
infinite blanket of stars? Or
are your memories more
accurately of the tedious
council estate shithole you
actually grew up in?

Gemini

The last six months have been
incredibly difficult for you but
you've emerged from them a
much more resilient character.
And given what the next six
months have in store, that's
going to be extraordinarily
useful.

Cancer

Minty. The next seven days are
going to be very, very...minty.

Leo

Okay, completely clear your mind of everything. Now I want you to imagine a place of total calm and tranquility. Can you see it? What colour does this place look like? Green? GREEN? Jesus, what's wrong with you? Green? Get the fuck away from me, you big freak.

Virgo

One, two buckle my shoe. Three, four knock on the door. Five, six sling your arse down the off-license and pick me up a shedload of Stella, there's a good chap.

Libra

Sometimes you just can't see the wood for the trees or, given what a filthy mind you've got, the muff for the pubes.

Scorpio

If petrol prices continue to rise at the same rate, there's a very real worry that you're not going to be able to afford to get pissed any more.

Sagittarius

As a ratified representative of the National Union Of Sages, Seers, Prognosticators and Sooths, I need to inform you that reading this horoscope constitutes crossing a recognised picket line.

Capricorn

I'll tell you what, I'll start thinking about the environment when it stops raining on me for nine bastard months of the year. Deal?

Aquarius

If only your friends could see you now. Actually, cart before the horse – if only you'd made some friends in the first place.

Pisces

Picking your nose and wiping it under the chair is a pretty disgusting habit and as a dentist you really should know better.

Aries

Lying in the park with your loved one, watching the clouds and saying what they look like, it's probably best not to point out the one that looks like a sobbing, sexually-frustrated woman who fears she's wasted the best years of her life on a feckless idiot. Say it looks like a tortoise or something.

Taurus

Negotiations for a pay rise start badly this week with your opening gambit of "Unless we can come to some other kind of arrangement, fuckboots?"

Gemini

Sometimes the sun goes round the moon, sometimes the snow falls down in June. And sometimes I wish I'd steered clear of the brown acid.

Cancer

Right now the world is your oyster, inasmuch as it smells fishy and has a good chance of making you vomit.

Leo

You want a woman that's a friend in the living room, a cook in the kitchen and a whore in the bedroom. So, a bearded Jamie Oliver lookalike that costs you two grand a week, then.

Scorpio

Your kids may find the anecdote about how you met their mother amusing, but the multi-angle DVD of how they were conceived may be going a little too far.

Virgo

Just remembering to switch off your computer every day can save as much as £50 a year on electricity. For your boss. Not selling this to you, am I?

Sagittarius

Your living situation improves for the first time since the divorce as the guys at the storage warehouse finally allow you to have a kettle in the container you've been living in.

Libra

After a bitter people's revolution that spread terror over ten years and saw thousands of innocent citizens executed, fast food fans are finally served their first Whopper Meal by the democratically-elected Burger President.

Capricorn

This week you work out some of the major flaws in current superconductor production theory that could fundamentally change their role in the computer industry, but forget to write them down because that video with the women doing aerobics comes on the telly.

Aquarius

Why not write a telly series
about vampires? Can't have too
many of them, can we?

Pisces

The police finally start to
become suspicious this week as
you 'find' your seventh body in
six months whilst walking your
dog. Maybe you should have
taken the knickers off
your head first?

Aries

Tuesday sees you come home
to find Saturn flicking through
your photo album, taking out
the occasional picture and
setting light to it with a Zippo
while laughing. Because, as
he calmly reminds you as a
memory of seaside childhood
becomes a plume of ash, he can.

Taurus

Your allergies include peanuts,
shellfish, wool, dairy products,
wheat and not being a fussy
little shit.

Gemini

Your story has been one of
tradition versus ambition,
as you turn your back on
the family business of seven
generations to carve out your
own fate in the world. And I
suppose not everybody's cut out
to be a pimp.

Cancer

Over the next weekend, you
will be called an arsehole on
no fewer than 47 occasions. It
would have been a whole lot
more but your uncle couldn't
make the funeral.

♌ Leo

A nice relaxing bath with some aromatic essential oils will be the perfect way to unwind at the end of the week. It may also get rid of that mackerel-y smell, too.

♍ Virgo

It's a beautifully-shot meditation on the fragile but eternal beauty of nature and the minutiae of human relationships set against the epic backdrop of the Alaskan mountains. Which is why you're going to watch van Damme's *Universal Soldier 3* instead.

Libra

Neither a borrower nor a lender be, for loan oft loses both itself and friend, and, in Bermondsey Dave's case, both your thumbs.

♏ Scorpio

Spam emails that say you can save over £300 on your home insurance are especially pointless when you don't actually own £300 worth of things.

Sagittarius

Bad news from the adoption agency after you asked whether they had any non-union ones that could work twelve-hour shifts.

Capricorn

If an infinite number of monkeys were sat for an infinite amount of time in front of an infinite number of typewriters, it would probably smell like your bedroom.

Aquarius

You're completely over your ex-girlfriend, in a strictly literal sense since, unbeknownst to her, you've moved into her attic.

Pisces

You cannot imagine what's going to happen to you this week, and afterwards you cannot imagine eating soup without half of it ending up in your lap.

Aries

Friends have come to realise you're not the best person to come to for love-life advice when most of your tips start with "Relationships are a lot like badger-baiting."

Taurus

Watching Mark Ronson on the decks, Brad & Angelina on the dance floor and the Cristal flow like water, you realise that millions of people would kill to be in this nightclub alongside you. As long as they didn't have to clean out the shitters like you do, of course.

Gemini

You schedule a meeting with HR after your boss instigates a new team-building exercise called 'Bring photos of your teenaged daughter to work Friday'.

Cancer

Torn between two lovers, feeling like a fool. The quantity of cock is pretty delightful, though.

Leo
Hello, my name is Inigo Montoya. You killed my father. Thanks for that, he was a right old prick.

Virgo
A nice back rub, a foot massage or even just a cuddle can be lovely ways to feel close to your lover without it having to mean sex is on the cards. But she always has to pressure you into it, doesn't she?

Libra
A trip around IKEA, with its cheap, collapsible furniture that looks initially appealing but ultimately tawdry, proves too heavy-handed a metaphor for your relationship this week. Good job it wasn't the municipal tip, really.

Scorpio
Your application to appear on *Snog, Marry Or Avoid?* is turned down after the producer's refusal to add an additional category of "Scare Away With Fire".

Sagittarius
Oscar Wilde often said that the easiest way to get rid of a temptation was to yield to it, but this week you'll find that imprisonment in a sex offender's unit will serve equally as well.

Capricorn
Your new surround sound speakers are so amazing it does sound like there's people sat behind your couch whispering into your ear. Only these voices aren't telling you to do something awful to next door's dog.

Aquarius

You like old movies. Like *The Godfather III*. Which is why you're going to spend the rest of your life alone. Arse.

Taurus

This week you realise you've got your TV on too loud when Graham Norton opens the central locking on your car.

Pisces

The ancient and arcane forces of the netherworld have been summoned forth by the wisdom of my magick brethren and apparently you're going to bump into an old friend this week. Fancy that.

Gemini

You're still scarred by a childhood dogged by the worst anti-Semitic bullying in the history of King David's School, Mount Sinai.

Cancer

Despite claiming to have an exhaustive selection of products, FunkyPigeon.com don't appear to have a 'Make another one of those twatting adverts and I'll hunt you down like a war criminal' card.

Aries

"The lady doth protest too much, methinks" is a poor closing argument in your sexual harassment case.

Leo

Go to Morocco. There you will meet a man named Hassan who will ask whether you enjoy the works of Proust. He will drive you to the foothills of the Q'altar mountains. At the summit is a man that, legend has it, knows how to stop Windows downloading updates.

Scorpio

That well-spoken chap who's been helping out at the shelter where you work turns out not to be, as you'd hoped, from *The Secret Millionaire* but from the dole office as part of a new show called *The Secret Investigation Into Non-Declaration of Voluntary Work*.

Virgo

It's always embarrassing when you wake up on the top deck of a number 82 in the bus terminal, still pissed as a rat. Not least because you're going to have to ask the driver for directions to work.

Sagittarius

If you're getting funny looks while playing frisbee with your dog in the park, remember that you don't both have to catch it with your mouth.

Libra

Oscar nominations are never going to sell a film to you until the Academy enter the 21st century and create an award for "Best Topless Car Chase".

Capricorn

Life is a tale told by an idiot, full of sound and fury, signifying nothing. Sort of like Justin Lee Collins reading *American Psycho* on *Jackanory*.

> *Your honesty is tested to the limit this week when you find a wallet full of money on the pavement. Do you take it and run, or do you wait with the old bloke who dropped it until the ambulance arrives?*

Aries

Famous Aryan: Jocky Wilson

Health:
Oral hygiene is going to be a paramount concern over the next 12 months, and it's about time you sorted out that filthy fucking mouth of yours.

Career:
Your parents have tears in their eyes as, standing proudly to attention with your uniform smartly pressed, you accept those pips that indicate your years of loyal service. One day you could be running a Subway of your own.

Romance:
Love isn't all about flowers, candlelight and expensive gifts. Sometimes it's about the little things in life like not calling them "Shit-for-brains" when they forget to flush the loo.

Highlight Of The Year:
Coming home to find the builder banging away at your wife like a Dave Grohl drum solo. Should knock at least 20% off his estimate. Jackpot.

Your Lucky One-Hit Wonder:
Funky Town - Lipps Inc

Aquarius

As a child, you couldn't
get enough of *Bedknobs &
Broomsticks*. Of course, these
days it's all anal love beads.
And still, to be fair, bedknobs.

Pisces

Your expenses claims are
unlikely to hit the headlines,
consisting mainly as they do of
pile cream and false eyelashes.

Aries

A visit to Alcoholics
Anonymous reminds you of
all the things you've done in
the past to get a drink, as well
as some things you'd never
have imagined doing. You're
definitely going to have a crack
at that off-license scam this
weekend.

Taurus

Remember, there are some
things you should never
write for yourself and those
are Valentine's cards, work
references and your own
nickname. Suicide notes?
Absolutely fine.

Gemini

Universal Pictures seem
completely uninterested in your
pitch for a romcom based on the
chalk-and-cheese relationship
between an embalmer and his
patient called *You've Got To
Formaldehyde Your Love Away*.

Cancer

I want to be loved by you, just
you and nobody else but you. I
want to be loved by you alone.
Boopboopbedoop. So what's the
Saint Bernard doing here?

Leo

That sudden hush when you walk into the room at work isn't respect, it's because your staff are breathing through their mouths to avoid the smell. Worked out why they call you 'The Big Cheese' yet?

Virgo

If you're writing the poster for a West End show this week, when using the phrase "Beg, steal or borrow a ticket", why not add the word "buy" into the sentence?

Libra

No, I'm sure that was one of JLS that took you around the back of Argos the other night and cut your evening short because he had to catch the last bus home. Just like that time half of The Wanted took you into the bogs in Nandos.

Scorpio

You're pretty sure you've seen *Inception, Jacob's Ladder* and *Memento* but there's always the chance you've...oh, you get the idea.

Sagittarius

Press Alt, Ctrl, Tab, Enter and Esc at the same time - something rather amazing happens. You realise how astoundingly gullible you are. Go on – microwave your phone, it'll be awesome, I promise.

Capricorn

Looking down into the toilet bowl, you see a stool in the perfectly-formed shape of Gillian McKeith. You're positive this means something but you're not entirely sure what.

Aquarius

I'm sure everyone is convinced that you shave your head because it's fashionable. And that's the same grunting noise Tinie Tempah makes when he gets out of a chair, right?

Taurus

Pipe, slippers, newspaper and a forty-minute visit to the cludgie. If it was good enough for your mum, it's good enough for your missus.

Pisces

Two weeks with nothing but the azure blue sky, the gently lapping waves and the burnished copper sun for company. Surely somebody will have noticed that the boat sank by now?

Gemini

Every atom of every molecule in your body was forged in the unimaginable furnace of the centre of a star and billions of years later the bits in your eyes are being used to read the *Daily Mail*.

Aries

A visit to the zoo is cut short this week after you're caught climbing into the meerkat enclosure and demanding they start singing *Hakuna Matata* or you want your money back.

Cancer

Your OCD moves into a fascinating territory this week as you arrange the stationery on your desk in the order of their allegiance to Beelzebub.

Leo

Many people use sampled film clips as their mobile ringtone, but not many decide to go with the pinball machine scene from *The Accused.*

Virgo

Simply scratch off this horoscope to reveal the prize underneath. Please be aware there's a strong possibility it could be a back-to-front horoscope.

Libra

Clearing out the spare room this weekend, you uncover the reason why you've had three tins of unused cat food at the back of the cupboard for the last six months.

Scorpio

A haiku sure is
A classy way for your doc
To say you've got crabs.

Sagittarius

Your attempts to initiate sex reach a new low this week after you try to draw attention to the whole area by colouring in your junk with a highlighter pen.

Capricorn

After an armed robbery goes pear-shaped, your sex life for the next eight to twelve years is about to get unpleasantly banana-shaped.

Aquarius

Forced to leave your stuck-up prep school and go to a run-down college in the 'hood, your fellow classmates teach you valuable life lessons, such as what it feels like to be beaten until you piss blood and what it's like to live in a constant state of crippling terror.

Pisces

After a horrible day at work, all you want is for him to gather you in his arms and tell you that everything's going to be okay. But he's all "Please buy something or get out of my off-license, sir." The swine.

Aries

To dream the impossible dream, to fight the unbeatable foe, to bear the unbearable sorrow, to run where the brave dare not go? Fuck that.

Taurus

With the world due to end in 2012 I can only repeat my advice of last week and recommend you continue drinking yourself into a renal coma before the fire-breathing warthogs show up.

Gemini

Doctors say that stroking a cat for just 20 minutes can reduce stress levels by 50%. Especially your cat, whose fur is thick with years of second-hand ganja smoke. It's like a hairy hash cake.

Cancer

Who says supermarkets can't offer the personal touch? Your local Asda has your value pizza, bottle of own-brand vodka and 10 Sovereign ready for you 10 o' clock every morning.

Leo

Home brew is an excellent way to beat the credit crunch, as well as eradicating the need for fibre in your diet.

Virgo

Yes you're right of course, anti-Welsh sentiments seem to be the last form of acceptable mainstream racism. Although to be more accurate, it's a form of species-ism, you incomprehensible, misshapen dwarf.

Libra

After initially diagnosing you with panic attacks, your GP has looked deeper at your life and renamed them "Startling moments of accurate clarity into the utter awfulness of your existence".

Scorpio

Ever the adventurous chef, you name your latest curry recipe 'Frodo', as it destroys the ring in a hellish inferno after an arduous ordeal that takes about ten hours.

Sagittarius

Your regular claim to support "The finest team the world has ever seen" would only possibly be true if success were measured by the number of arrests for racially-aggravated assaults. And even then, half of La Liga would give you solid competition.

Capricorn

Police finally catch up with you after you file duct tape, shovels and 50kg of quicklime on your tax return as deductible business expenses.

Aquarius

While you've never believed in the supernatural, you're given cause to reconsider this week when 16 successive clicks on Wikipedia's 'Random Article' link brings up the same page describing the details of your horrifically violent death next Tuesday.

Pisces

Your twelve-bet accumulator depends on getting the right result on Saturday, but given the fact you've bet against the universe crushing your dreams in an hilariously timely fashion, I wouldn't start spending the winnings just yet.

Aries

Shall I compare thee to a summer's day? One in Blackpool in the midst of a hen party, perhaps?

Taurus

Cut the green wire. Or is it the blue wire? Blue? Yes, yes blue. Definitely blue. NO WAIT, is it green? Oh fuck it, just buy a new kettle instead.

Gemini

Your other half is unimpressed with your attempt at getting your life in order when you present him with a Powerpoint presentation detailing what order you'd do Take That in with an explanatory handout. Gary last, obviously.

Cancer

Life's a lot more complicated than in the movies, as you discover this week when an attempt to recreate *Weekend At Bernie's* ends up requiring a lot more Febreze than you're making in fraudulent benefit claims.

Leo

Hath not a Jew eyes? Hath not a Jew hands, organs, dimensions, senses, affections, passions; fed with the same food, hurt with the same weapons, subject to the same diseases, heal'd by the same means, warm'd and cool'd by the same winter and summer, as a Christian is? Let the *Daily Mail* know what YOU think on this issue.

Virgo

No, I don't think completing *Space Dungeon* on the Atari really does put you in the running to succeed Steve Jobs, actually.

Libra

Bad news ahead as you discover you have diabetes when the sugar in your urine causes your golden shower slave to go into a diabetic coma.

Scorpio

Just a perfect day. Feed animals in the zoo, then later a movie too and then home. Where we'll take a quite frankly staggering amount of smack.

Sagittarius

Yes it does look like Alan Sugar with a hangover, you're right. Now put it away, for Christ's sake.

Capricorn

I'll send you all my love every day in a letter. And seal it with…well, you can probably guess that.

In your youth you may have dabbled with all manner of psychotropic drugs and opiates but these days you're much happier with a quiet night in, a nice glass of merlot and a magazine of heartstopping Japanese pornography.

Taurus

Famous Taurasaur: Nikki Grahame

Health:
Not a great year as you're going to be a martyr to hoof-rot and cracked udder through the summer, so that's wearing a bikini out of the question.

Career:
You manage to secure a loan from your bank's small business advisor for your latest venture - a shakedown operation threatening small business advisors in return for loans.

Romance:
You can remember your first boyfriend, your first kiss, losing your virginity and your first broken heart because they all conveniently happened within 12 minutes of each other at Holly Turnbull's 16th birthday party.

Highlight Of The Year:
Being at home every time the councillors doorknock during the local election and watching them squirm for 20 minutes when you ask what they're going to do to make the neighbourhood "A bit less sambo".

Your Lucky One-Hit Wonder: Hey Mickey - Toni Basil

Aquarius

You finally show the world your musical talent deserves a wider audience as Ebbsfleet Double Glazing Warehouse commission a radio jingle from you.

Taurus

You have to move with the times and finally trade in your Gaydar for the latest in Satellite Navigaytion.

Gemini

You manage to outfox your work's internet tracking department by surfing pornography so outlandishly outré that they're too embarrassed to describe it in a report.

Pisces

Nothing ruins a long train journey more than a screaming child for the whole trip. That's the last time you'll forget to put ouzo in their bottle.

Aries

While nobody can truly claim to know the vagaries of the human heart, I think it's a fairly safe bet that you're not going to win her back by screaming Iron Maiden lyrics down the phone at her at two in the morning.

Cancer

You want to warn people in your email that you're about to give away the ending of the film where somebody is decapitated by the aerodynamic modification on the back of a car, but can't think of a suitable phrase for it.

Leo

If life is a pie and success is the crust, then your recent endeavours are…erm…the suet of effort and…okay, I've not really thought this one through, to be honest.

Virgo

Cruising down the Texas highway in the hot August sun with a preacher testifying some of that old-time religion on the radio, you realise you must have taken a wrong turning for Homebase at the Slough interchange.

Libra

Your terrible sense of direction is confirmed this week as you get lost in the map section of Waterstones.

Scorpio

Men's emotional and sexual responses are complexly interwoven and care should be taken when asking your boyfriend to share his innermost thoughts. But giving him a chewie while the football's on will almost certainly brighten his day.

Sagittarius

An amazing week for you, filled with celebrations, romantic interest, mone…hang on, those aren't stars, they're bits of sugar off my doughnut. Let me just clear those away and…oh dear, more infected boils, I'm afraid.

Capricorn

What part of 'Piss off' don't you understand? Oh, désolé, je ne savais pas. Je vous demande simplement de faire chier.

Aquarius

Your bedsit is 10' by 10' by 8' and the sum volume of your furniture is 320 cubic feet, meaning it would take the innards of 829,440 Creme Eggs to fill it to the brim. Calculations such as those are the things you use to while away your existence.

Taurus

After receiving several unsolicited sales calls of an evening whilst at home, you really stick it to The Man this week by hurling abuse at some poor minimum-wage bastard trying to earn a living just like the rest of us. Take THAT, capitalism.

Pisces

Bolivian, 100% pure, with a street value of £20,000 a kg. The price of organic coffee is absolutely scandalous these days, isn't it?

Gemini

Eye of newt and toe of frog, wool of bat and tongue of dog. Also contains monosodium glutamate and processed in a facility that may have contained peanuts.

Aries

After Liverpool University granted their first MA in The Beatles earlier this year, this week you become the proud recipient of Carlisle Technical College's first City & Guilds in Roxanne Pallett.

Cancer

Sometimes, when people are suffering extreme grief it's difficult to find the right words to say, so why not try sock puppetry or a pop-up book full of frowny faces?

Leo

Don't worry, it's a routine operation that the surgeon has performed hundreds of times before, although possibly not just after he's found out his wife is having an affair. With you. You don't need both kidneys, though, right?

Virgo

Pineapple and cinnamon are just two foods proven to improve the taste of your semen, although you could just stop using it as a margarine substitute.

Libra

Get that celeb vibe for your next party by inviting 300 people you don't know, not letting any of them in and sitting on your couch looking completely miserable all night

Scorpio

In such a depressed property market, you're surprised this week when Channel 4 turn down your pitch for *Kirsty & Phil's Arson Insurance Scams*.

Sagittarius

Remember, only losers take drugs. Losers and incredibly creative, vibrant, successful people who live more in one day than you manage in a decade. And we both know which camp you'd fall in, don't we?

Capricorn

University shouldn't just be about getting a qualification, it should be about expanding your mind to new experiences, like living amongst six other people's filth and having everybody really fucking hate you.

Aquarius

You've started taking a banana
into work to help with one
of your five a day. And you
could always eat the banana
afterwards.

Pisces

A difficult conversation this
week as you try and explain to
your child why pets sometimes
die. How can a four year-old
fully grasp complex concepts
like not being arsed to keep
cleaning up after a furry little
shitbag?

Aries

Beware, my Lord, of jealousy
– it is the green ey'd monster
which doth mock the meat it
feeds on. A bit like that time
you went to that city farm and
called the pig a pudgy, pink
nobhead.

Taurus

In a desperate attempt to cram
every stag weekend activity into
one afternoon, this Saturday
you'll find yourself shooting
paintballs at a stripper from a
moving go-kart.

Gemini

Your parents passed their own
irrational fears onto you as a
toddler, but given that was in
the early 80s you should be fine
as long as you don't bump into
anyone wearing a calculator
watch and legwarmers. Avoid
Carlisle.

Cancer

Granted, the holiday you
booked this week was a bargain.
But website photos of a hotel
shouldn't really have a NSFW
warning, should they?

Leo

Itunes need to stop being
so strait-laced – you're
positive there'd be a huge
market for an App like
FindMyDoggingCarpark.

Virgo

A good rule of thumb during
a Spring clean is to throw
anything out that you haven't
used for over a year, but I don't
know how you're going to
dump your libido in the bin.

Libra

It's your 20th anniversary
school reunion this week – with
a full head of hair and a brace
of spent convictions, you'll
be viewed as quite the social
climber.

Scorpio

You're a maverick big-city cop
sent to a sleepy small town to
investigate a string of murders
and your unconventional ways
soon start ruffling feathers
amongst the stuffy elders.
And following a lengthy
investigation by the Police
Complaints Commission
you're reassigned to back office
administrative duties until
further notice.

Sagittarius

And we can build this dream
together, standing tall forever,
nothing's gonna stop us now.
Pending planning permission.

Capricorn

This week you're thrown out of
a production of *Der Fliegende
Holländer* for heckling the tenor
playing Erik to "Do the one off
the Go Compare adverts".

Aquarius

So it's another week sleeping on the couch for joking to your wife that it's always artificial insemination if you pretend you're still in love with her during sex.

Pisces

Your life coach commends you on your personal growth after he uses the word 'do' twice in a sentence and you don't even giggle.

Aries

If you gathered together every person you'd ever kissed in your life, let alone slept with, it wouldn't even be enough to conduct a satisfactory cosmetics survey. That mental image is my gift to you this week.

Taurus

Can you hear us, pumping on your stereo? Can you hear us, pumping on your stereo? Not since about 1999, lads, no.

Gemini

Nutritionists always recommend that you should watch what you eat, but that's going to be harder than it sounds with a staggering overbite like yours.

Cancer

Money, money, money. Must be funny, in a rich man's world. Especially when they fish for tramps using fivers as bait.

Leo
You really enjoyed Martin Luther King's biography, feeling kinship with his amazing civil rights work after that time you clicked 'like' on somebody's Facebook post criticising Jim Davidson.

Virgo
Drinking in moderation every night shouldn't pose any risk to your health, but for the fact 'moderation' is the name of a local bar where Polish fishermen drink bathtub-distilled potato schnapps.

Libra
Recognition at last for your continued custom as the preservation order on your local pub requires that any alterations must include your bar stool.

Scorpio
I'm no employment expert but I'm pretty sure that a job contract can't include under "any other duties" the requirement to "Get yo freak on wit yo line manager".

Sagittarius
You're going to come back from your year of backpacking a completely different person – right now you're a prick that doesn't have malaria or a suntan.

Capricorn
Won't you take me to, a funky town? Won't you take me to, a funky town? Watch out for the one-way system this time of night, though.

> **"**
> *A proud moment for you*
> *this week as you manage to*
> *text everybody a weak pun*
> *you've assembled, based on a*
> *catastrophic event, before most*
> *of the bereaved families have*
> *even been told their relative has*
> *died. No, you're the hero.*
> **"**

Gemini

Famous Geminum:
Bobcat Goldthwait

Health:
I don't want to alarm you but a severe downturn in your health toward the end of the year will be made to look like an accident.

Career:
You neither live to work nor work to live at the moment. "Work to keep yourself in crystal meth" just about covers it.

Romance:
You've managed to keep the passion going after all these years because of what you bring to the relationship. He brings the Viagra and you bring the schnapps.

Highlight Of The Year:
Managing to go 12 months without having to use the phrase "Not guilty, your honour".

Your Lucky One-Hit Wonder:
Cotton-Eyed Joe - Rednex

Aquarius

I don't think anyone's falling for that story where you try fending off a ketchup-bottle-wielding burglar by dropping your trousers and farting at him. Just be honest with the A&E nurse. She's probably seen it before.

Taurus

When your daughter's boyfriend asks why you resent him so much, ask him to imagine he's spent 18 years building an E-type Jag only to see it being driven off by some numpty that's only just learned how to drive.

Pisces

Here's a cure for the travel sickness you interminably inflict on anybody who'll listen during long journeys. It involves nailing big crooked planks of wood over your front door.

Gemini

Caciocavallo Podolico cheese, made in the hills of Southern Italy from the milk of wild cows, is incredibly rare, with just 1kg made every season. And makes a fucking lousy cheese on toast.

Aries

Let me be absolutely clear on one thing. Because I'm going to be all vague and mystic and generally shit about everything else.

Cancer

The producers regret inviting you onto *Saturday Kitchen* after you tell them your "food hell" is "anything cooked by Jews".

Leo

I must say, it was very brave of you to go into the hairdressers and ask for the "crack whore on her day off" look. What? Oh, sorry.

Virgo

When explaining the facts of life to your kids, make sure you use loads of hand gestures and noises. It would be embarrassing for them to have nothing to tell the therapists in 20 years' time.

Libra

Having Sky TV has made such a difference. Now it takes 45 minutes to flick through the channels before deciding there's fuck-all on.

Scorpio

Exciting times this week as the BBC green-light your more aggressive genealogy program *Who Do You Think You Are Looking At?*

Sagittarius

You've not been feeling especially Zen recently after your crystal therapist accused your homeopath of bolloxing up your chakras and your Reiki healer ended up twatting the both of them. And the scuffle completely arsed up the Feng Shui in your flat.

Capricorn

A chance visit to a standup comedy gig leads you to the startling discovery that Nigerian parents are very strict and speak in quite pronounced accents.

Aquarius

While the banging 2-step breakbeat and dutty basslines of grime make the heart race, one cannot help but return to the wicked bpm and braaap of speed garage. Don't you find?

Pisces

Have you tried switching it off then switching it on again? I'll be honest, I'm no expert on life-support machines.

Aries

What a piece of work is a man, how noble in reason, how infinite in faculties, in form and moving how express and admirable, in action how like an angel, in apprehension how like a god! Shame about the dangly bollocks, though.

Taurus

Due to further government savings, your star sign will close down for one week a year to cut costs. But do you think anything interesting is going to happen to you that you need to know about? Really?

Gemini

It's a sign of your growing maturity as you approach middle age that your workplace nickname has stopped referring to your tits and started referring to your droopy arse. Progress, of a kind.

Cancer

For he's a jolly good fellow, for he's a jolly good fellow, for he's a joll...really? Over 20,000 images on his hard drive? Oh dear.

Leo
Your holiday to Mumbai sparks a diplomatic crisis this week as you're arrested for strolling around dressed as Clive Of India, sticking Post-It notes on everything saying 'Property of The Queen'.

Virgo
When Andy leaves his bedroom, his toys come to life and have all kinds of crazy adventures. In their latest, they try and bust Andy out of the psychiatric ward after he walks in while they're having a meeting and goes shit-flinging mental.

Libra
You have earned a Playstation Network Trophy for *Call Of Duty IV*: "Completely disregard your personal hygiene for an entire week".

Scorpio
You've done a lot of good work in the local community recently. Just 120 hours to go before you can hand the orange jumpsuit back.

Sagittarius
You've got to hold and give, but do it at the right time. You can be slow or fast, but you must get to the line. They'll always hit you and hurt you, defend and attack. There's only one way to beat them, get round the back. Or get your arses handed to you in the quarter finals. Y'know, whatever works for you.

Capricorn
You can pop as many cherries and umbrellas in it as you want, but your home-made mix of rubbing alcohol and lemon Fairy Liquid is not a 'cocktail'.

Aquarius

Spring is definitely in the air as the daffodils bloom, the birdsong returns and you become so priapic you'd cheerfully hump a letter box if you stuck a wig on it.

Pisces

After years of setting you targets which are 'SMART' (Specific, Measurable, Achievable, Realistic & Timely), your boss decides to try some that are DUMB (Deliberately Unachievable, you Miserable Bastard).

Aries

If you're stuck for a last-minute costume for a fancy dress party, just turn up, slap every woman there on the arse and if anybody asks, you're Andy Gray.

Taurus

I agree that it takes less than 10 minutes to make your own mayonnaise from scratch but it takes less than 10 seconds for me to call you a pretentious wanker. And I know which is more enjoyable

Gemini

First the storm knocked the phone and power cables out, then that creepy old book started making unearthly moaning noises and now there's some weird kind of creaking coming from downstairs. Could you go and see what it is? Otherwise I won't get a wink of sleep.

Cancer

Time to lose weight as your friend decides that you count as your own +1 on the wedding invite he sent.

Leo

You've often wondered – if they advertised Milky Bar with albino kids, why didn't they advertise the Curly Wurly with Spina Bifida kids? And this is why you're never invited anywhere.

Virgo

Happiness, happiness, the greatest gift that I possess, apart from a cock that looks like an ostrich's neck wrapped in raw bacon.

Libra

After many weeks of careful planning, you manage to fulfil the request in Paddy McGuinness' Saturday night show using a sniper rifle. No like-y, no room for second chances by going for the head shot-y.

Scorpio

Cowards die many times before their deaths; the valiant never taste of death but once, but that's usually in a hail of bullets wondering who set them on fire

Sagittarius

Taking out your acoustic guitar at a party this weekend really draws a crowd as people queue up to watch you being beaten unconscious with it.

Capricorn

Imagine a situation where a fat, shouty man in his 40s acting like a 12-year-old would be really inappropriate, leading to all kinds of chaos. An operating theatre, perhaps. Or a funeral parlour. Got it? Congratulations, you've just saved yourself £10, two hours and the need to see the next Will Ferrell movie.

Aquarius
You regret asking Saturn whether half of the money now and half next week will be okay after he asks whether half of the dog now and half next week will be okay.

Pisces
Your blind date describes himself as "Cheeky, fun-loving, doesn't take life too seriously and always up for a laugh". You know. An idiot.

Aries
Don't feel guilty about not attending to your spiritual side, when you've lived a good life of quiet philanthropy like yours, any half-decent creator would reserve a place for you in heaven. You'd have to be a sadistic lunatic to think otherwise. Or a Methodist.

Taurus
Your biggest vice is a big takeaway curry and a six-pack of beer on a Friday night but, given that your biggest vice used to involve a claw hammer, park bushes and infinite patience, you're not going to start feeling bad about it.

Gemini
After appearing in the latest Webuyanycar advert, people might finally stop talking about that nursery you managed that got closed down by the police.

Cancer
This week, you have a bad first day as a Palestinian negotiator with your opening gambit of "Who would want to live in a shithole like this anyway?"

Leo

It's with an air of sadness that you leave this week's Robert Plant gig, your heart heavy in the knowledge that he's beginning to look like Aslan's piss-artist older brother.

Virgo

You're not one of those unrealistic brides that wants everything to be fairytale perfect but you do feel you're within your rights to complain when the groom turns up with his breath smelling like prossie.

Libra

In the current economic climate, negotiations with Satan over the value of your immortal soul go badly and you end up in negative equity, needing to find a further three souls per year to avoid being repossessed.

Scorpio

Top marks for originality after you open a furniture store whose motto is "Pay the full price or piss off out the shop".

Sagittarius

To you, it's the holiday cruise of a lifetime. To everyone else it's two weeks trapped in the middle of the ocean in an overpriced Butlins with 3,000 of the worst examples of the terrible ravages age can wreak on the human body and soul. Bon voyage!

Capricorn

Ayeupdoestheewantafucking-pintlad? AlreetsonI'mgannak nackyouinthaplums. Life in a Northern Town...

Aquarius

You just can't understand why you were kicked off the stage of *Britain's Got Talent*. You'd like to see them try doing that with two live ferrets and a jar of peanut butter.

Pisces

What's in a name? That which we call a rose by any other name would smell as sweet. So just eat your dungcrackers and shut up.

Aries

It's taken thousands of doctors thousands of years to even begin understanding how the human body works, but no – I'm sure that cure your Nan came up with will work just fine.

Taurus

How about having a quiet night in on your own for a change? Rather than those heartbreakingly quiet nights out you've been having, where you sit alone at a pub table and your only conversation is to tell people that no, nobody's using that chair. Change as good as a rest and all that.

Gemini

This week you promise to give your boss 110% at work. You really are the world's shittest accountant.

Cancer

You've always had an old head on young shoulders, giving you the appearance of a midget wearing a Michael Douglas mask.

Leo

One last check to make sure you've got everything for your holiday to Spain – passport, tickets, luggage, utter contempt for everything foreign – yep, you're good to go.

Scorpio

Your wife complains that you put her up on a pedestal, but how else is she going to get into the loft to lag the boiler and kill that massive bat?

Virgo

There's hints that the feud between you and your neighbour seems to be calming down as you wake to find only the rear windscreen of your car smeared in excrement. It's a foul-smelling olive branch of sorts.

Sagittarius

Never go to sleep with an argument unresolved. Resort to arm-wrestling if necessary, although she does have the weight advantage.

Libra

Who's the black private dick that's a sex machine to all the chicks? And can you explain exactly why he's texting you at two in the morning about what a complicated man he is?

Capricorn

Really? St Crispin, you say? Can we hold off the battle until it's a saint that sounds a little less gay? I've written a whole speech and it'd be a shame to waste it.

> **"**
>
> *In a world where deeds speak louder than words, it's always better to act. Unless you're Eddie Izzard, in which case it's not.*
>
> **"**

Cancer

Famous Tumour:
Clarissa Dickson-Wright

Health:
You're so, so brave.

Career:
Realigning your core business objectives, streamlining your third-party service level agreements and aggressively targeting your competitor's weakest customer base could see you ride the financial storm this year. Or just buy a bastard big can of petrol.

Romance:
Your years of being single are going to change in the next 12 months as you smoothly progress from 'carefree singleton' to 'tragic spinster' in the time it takes to buy a cardigan.

Highlight Of The Year:
Finding that case of out-of-date Supernoodles behind Iceland.

Your Lucky One-Hit Wonder:
Because I Got High - Afroman

Aquarius

Yes, a seven-foot Austrian built like a brick shithouse is the perfect design to infiltrate the human resistance. Why not attach a pair of wings to his back and a two-foot luminous cock to his forehead while you're at it?

Pisces

Still no word from the BBC as to when they're releasing their *Points Of View* Blu Ray box set. The extras are going to be awesome.

Aries

This week at work you'll face an agonising wait of almost four minutes between saying "Well I never knew that" while reading your paper and a colleague finally relenting and asking "You never knew what?"

Taurus

Your romance has a fairytale ending this week as your boyfriend locks you in your own oven and murders your grandmother.

Gemini

The rapidly-rising unemployment figures absolutely infuriate you as you've been into being unemployed for years, way before it was popular. Next thing you know, everyone will be moving into poorly-maintained hostels.

Cancer

I said a hip hop, the hippie, the hippie to the hip hip hop a you don't stop the rock it to the bang bang boogie, say up jumped the boogie to the rhythm of the boogie, the beat. You heard me the first time.

♌
Leo
The Apple store fails to show its usual level of customer service after refusing to give you a refund on the shattered pieces of your iPhone, despite you patiently explaining what an overpriced, erratic, obdurate oblong of fuck it's been.

♍
Virgo
Your boasts down the pub that you had trials for Yorkshire Cricket Club would be more convincing if you didn't keep referring to your proficiency with the 'racquet'.

Libra
After browsing what the high streets shops have to offer, reading online reviews and consulting price comparison websites, you finally take the plunge and buy that five-pack of socks.

♏
Scorpio
Your latest boyfriend is like a movie idol from the golden age of Hollywood. An alcoholic, racist bisexual.

Sagittarius
Staring at the cold dawn sunrise, your face set into a grimace of determined resolve, you know in the depths of your soul that today is the day that you emerge from the ashes of your former life into a bright new future. Now if that doesn't warrant a three-day cider binge, I don't know what does.

♑
Capricorn
Your poor grasp of written English finally catches up with you this week as the police explain that you haven't actually been swapping emails with a child called Mo from Leicester.

Aquarius

The secret to really crispy roast potatoes and perfectly moist roast chicken is to entrust their cooking to somebody less cock-fingeredly useless than you.

Taurus

As far as you're concerned it's not really porn unless it leaves you feeling drained and slightly sordid – the same reason you always travel by National Express.

Pisces

To be honest, I think you have about three more chances to ask your Northern Irish colleague to say "How now brown cow" for a laugh before he goes bastard berserk at you.

Gemini

Like a lot of women, you claim to be able to tell a lot about a man by the shoes he wears, but using that logic you should have spent your whole life dating clowns.

Aries

All the world's a stage and all the men and women merely players. They have their exits and their entrances and one man in his time plays many parts. Apart from Sean Connery. He's always Scottish.

Cancer

That *Jamie's 30 Minute Meals* show certainly stopped you from ordering takeaway, because after watching him dribble away for half an hour you'd completely lost your appetite.

Leo

Jupiter is stood right in the front of your horoscope, saying there's nothing to see here and telling me to do one. I can see police lights over his shoulder and a SOCO officer putting something into an evidence bag. Yikes.

Virgo

You're suddenly struck this week by the astounding leaps forward technology has taken even in your lifetime, to such a degree that somebody from just 20 years ago woul....ooh, look a kitten falling over on YouTube! Ahahahaaaaaa.

Libra

They're a stuffy lot at your Beginner's Spanish evening class. All you wanted to know is how to say "Where all the pussy at?"

Scorpio

After living the billionaire playboy lifestyle for years, a life-changing incident convinces you to use your wealth and abilities to fight crime on the mean streets. But after having the paste beaten out of you by the first crackhead mugger you encounter, you're soon nipple-deep in Ferraris and supermodels once more.

Sagittarius

Now I've had the time of my life, no I never felt this way before. Yes I swear it's the truth and I owe it all to you. As well as £150, I think we said?

Capricorn

You realise your back hair has got out of control this week when you lean against some flock wallpaper and have to be cut free.

Aquarius

Annoy the beggar on the tube
by walking just slightly in front
of him, asking people if they
have a pound to spare so you
can get fucked up on schnapps.

Pisces

Why not spice up your sex life
by getting a treatment down
the beauty spa, putting on
some saucy underwear and a
revealing dress, then popping
out to a nightclub to find
somebody whose
cock works properly?

Aries

A dab of white vinegar on a
cloth will usually get rid of
most stains, but for a forensic
standard of cleanliness you're
better off burning the house
down and moving abroad.

Taurus

Training for the London
Marathon starts in earnest.
Step one – being able to fill in
the application form without
breaking into a sweat.

Gemini

Switching to recycled ink
cartridges can save you up
to £50 a year, but doing all
your printing at work can save
a lot more. The same logic
has always informed your
defecatory habits, too.

Cancer

You manage to spoil a romantic
walk along the beach this
weekend by trying to earn a bit
of money on the side by doing a
bit of cockle-picking.

Leo

That box you've moved from one house to the next for the past five years – at some point you're going to have to open it to see if the cat's still alive.

Virgo

Bad news – the laser eye clinic won't let you borrow their equipment to make your mate Tony go cross-eyed for a stag night stunt.

Libra

Your wardrobe is like a time capsule of what wasn't fashionable ten years ago and would be of great interest to bullying historians worldwide.

Scorpio

No matter how much of a rush you're in, love letters should never start with "To whom it may concern".

Sagittarius

If anyone asked you about your life 12 months ago, you'd tell them you were broke, lonely and without hope. But now you'd struggle to decide what to talk about first – your recent wedding, your exciting new career or your holiday to the Maldives. So give yourself a break and think how far you've come in the space of a year when it comes to bullshitting people about how happy you are.

Capricorn

Toga! Toga! Toga! Toga! To... oh, sorry, Togo? Erm, West Africa, I think.

Aquarius

As a lecturer you're used to people doodling or even texting as you work, but things go too far this week when a volleyball game breaks out.

Taurus

A pretty quiet Friday last weekend – you only had two or three before going home – but obviously you can't remember their names.

Pisces

You feel singled out as the crime stats are released for your street, mentioning just one incident of "Outraging public decency with a guide dog". Why don't they just print a photo of you and be done with it?

Gemini

You're a grizzled LA cop, sent to the perpetual daylight of Alaska to investigate a murder, and you've not been able to sleep for six days straight. Mostly due to fear that Robin Williams is suddenly going to leap out and start improvising at you.

Aries

Don't ask for a doggy bag at an all-you-can-eat buffet, as it might come across as slightly greedy.

Cancer

The man that hath no music in himself, nor is moved with concord of sweet sounds, is fit for treasons, stratagems and spoils. And that, I think you'll find, is proof that deaf people are evil.

Leo

If you started a chain of hotels by motorways that nobody would go to for their holiday and nobody would want to get pissed at, you probably wouldn't have called it Holiday Inn. But the bank won't give you a business loan for a company called Misery Wank Room.

Virgo

Tramps like us, baby we were born to run. Usually out of Asda with a bottle of vodka stuffed down our knickers.

Libra

At your forthcoming job interview, put your shoulders back, give a firm handshake, look them straight in the eye and let them know the Social forced you to apply for the job or they'd stop your dole.

Scorpio

At the end of your date, he gives you a charmingly old-world peck on the cheek and puts you into a cab, meaning you have to disconnect the camera equipment and the gimp swing in your flat alone.

Sagittarius

If symptoms persist after three days, consult your GP. Actually, you may as well call them now because it will take that long to get an appointment.

Capricorn

The next time somebody says a toddler is so cute they could just eat them all up, as a nursery nurse you really should avoid suggesting possible recipes.

Aquarius

When God closes a door, he
opens a window, proving that
he moves in a mysterious way
even when he's just nipping out
to the shops.

Pisces

The problem with being a
plumber is that, when the pipes
start leaking in your own home,
you have to go through the
whole rigmarole of repeatedly
lying to yourself and avoiding
your house for six weeks.

Aries

It may just be coincidence, but
as the progressive arthritis in
your hands has twisted your
index and middle finger around
each other, you've become a lot
more lucky.

Taurus

A worrying visit to the GP this
week as the gathering crowd
and 80" plasma TV in the
waiting room make you wonder
what precisely they mean by
'cervical screening'.

Gemini

After another Sunday morning
hangover featuring melting
clocks and lobster telephones,
you vow to lay off the
surreal ale.

Cancer

Researching your ancestry,
you're amazed to discover
you're not the only person in
your family to have been chased
out of Carlisle by hundreds of
torch-wielding locals with a
pig under one arm and lipstick
smeared across your face.
It's the circle of extremely
disturbing yokel life.

Leo

After killing a gangland rival by forcing an enormous trilby up his anus, your boss patiently explains the actual meaning of the phrase "pop a cap in his ass".

Virgo

Once upon a time you dressed so fine, threw the bums a dime in your prime, didn't you? Even though you knew dimes weren't legal tender over here. Prick.

Libra

You have an enjoyable night at the football booing a group of millionaires who couldn't give a shit, paying £4 for a meat pie the equivalent of a petri dish covered in pastry, and returning to find your car covered in more scratches than an Emo's arm. The beautiful game, innit?

Scorpio

You are the music and the music is you, the pill coursing through your veins has opened up your third eye and your friends are gonna be talking about a wicked night like this for the rest of their lives. Just ignore the arsehole security guard asking you to leave. Dixons is a public place, right?

Sagittarius

Are you sure you haven't had a stroke? You sound like Paul Whitehouse trying to do an accent.

Capricorn

Visiting your old friends who stayed behind in the small town where you grew up, you can't understand why they all think the big city has changed you. Calling them all 'boy' probably isn't helping.

> ## "
> *You've only yourself to blame*
> *for getting two years for*
> *describing the judge's eldest*
> *child as a miscarriage of justice.*
>
> ## "

Leo

Famous Leopard:
Danny La Rue

Health:
Come Christmas you're going to be amazed by the progress you've made in rehabilitative physiotherapy. What? Oh, nothing.

Career:
You work hard and play hard so as a fan of Bruce Willis you'll be pleased to hear that by the age of 41 the stress levels will cause you to die hard.

Romance:
Remember, holding hands and cuddling need not necessarily lead to sex. It could be the prelude to a night of spectacular genital branding and scat worship.

Highlight Of The Year:
Answering a question on *University Challenge* and spending the next 30 minutes running around the living room with your grimy t-shirt pulled over your head.

Your Lucky One-Hit Wonder:
Shaddap You Face - Joe Dolce

Aquarius

Success at last this week when the Prime Minister phones you to say he's read your blog, had a bit of a think and decided to completely dismantle the apparatus of government and rebuild it along the lines you suggested.

Pisces

After finally understanding the difficult conflicting demands of geopolitics and acknowledging that your parents had your best interests at heart, you have to disband the gloom metal outfit you're currently fronting.

Aries

You've never understood the taboo around the word 'cunt' but your fellow gynaecologists seem to think it's inappropriate to use in front of patients. Bunch of cunts.

Taurus

My name is Maximus Decimus Meridius, Commander of the armies of the North, General of the Felix legions, loyal servant to the true Emperor, Marcus Aurelius. Father to a murdered son, husband to a murdered wife. My interests include long walks in the park and going to the cinema. WLTM similar.

Gemini

I don't think you can declare a Jihad if you're a white atheist, you know. And certainly not against a canteen for running out of curly fries.

Cancer

Everyone has that one secret about themselves that would ruin their life if it were ever made public, except for you. Because yours was just printed on the internet. Uh-oh.

♌ Leo

Taking to the stage with your ukelele and your humorous poem about the Pre-Raphaelites going to a McDonalds, you sense a certain tension in the audience of 300 squaddies that have paid £10 to just have a laugh, thanks very much. Turn up the fey, surrealist whimsy – that should get them smiling.

♍ Virgo

You pride yourself on being Metrosexual after having a wank in a city centre branch of Tesco

Libra

As the sound of doors bolting shut ring out behind you, the dread realisation sinks in that this film features large amounts of Jude Law. Time to set light to the seats and hope the fire brigade can rescue you.

♏ Scorpio

When asked by your friends how you've kept your relationship alive for 20 years, your other half talks about mutual respect, shared values and a sense of commitment. Better think of something better than "staying half-pissed most of the time" before it's your turn.

Sagittarius

It's Chinese, early 19th century, probably from the Gansu province, made from bamboo and cherrywood and I'm buggered if I'm going to eat it.

Capricorn

What? Another photo of your cat sleeping, you say? Quick, get me to a computer ASAP so I can get on Facebook and take a look at this. Jesus.

Aquarius

I love that you get cold when it's 71 degrees out. I love that it takes you an hour and a half to order a sandwich. I love that you get a little crinkle above your nose when you're looking at me like I'm nuts. I love that after I spend the day with you, I can still smell your perfume on my clothes. And I love that you are the last person I want to talk to before I go to sleep at night. You also have excellent charlies.

Pisces

Unable to afford a mail-order bride, this week you pay your first instalment on a wank you've bought from a catalogue.

Aries

Under neon loneliness, motorcycle emptiness. Nope, I've no idea either.

Taurus

Nabokov managed to write *Pale Fire* in his second language while you can't write a shopping list in your first language without popping a stray apostrophe into the word 'eggs'.

Gemini

By the time you'd finished watching your box set of *The Wire* you were talking like a Baltimore hood-rat despite being from Bradford. Let's see what happens with *Queer As Folk*.

Cancer

A difficult time for you as you're unable to tell your followers that the demonstration at the birth control clinic is cancelled due to your squeamishness with the whole 'A' word.

Leo

Asked about the progress of the project assigned to you six weeks ago, you're a little embarrassed to admit the only thing you've got to show for it is the ability to play *Waltzing Mathilda* by twanging your ruler on your desk. Ask for a fortnight's extension and you'll get *Good Vibrations* under your belt, too.

Virgo

There's a fine line between Kung Fu and just running around in your pyjamas, shouting at people.

Libra

You discover a money-making scheme with *World Of Warcraft* fans by offering to knock shite out of them with a sword for half the usual price of a subscription.

Scorpio

If he's stalling over having kids, tell him that you ARE going to gain four stone and become an unbearable mess in the near future. Whether that involves pregnancy or not is entirely up to him.

Sagittarius

Last month you put a notebook by the bed to record any ideas you may have and so far it contains nothing but the phrase 'Have a wank' 26 times.

Capricorn

If wearing headphones and keeping your eyes downcast won't stop that person on the bus talking to you, try pretending you're a born-again Christian. They'll probably leap out of the window, which will piss Jesus off no end.

Aquarius

I want to be the one you turn to in times of trouble and the one who cheers the loudest in your times of triumph. A true friend and the one who knows you better than you know yourself. But most of all I want to warm my nose up between your knockers.

Taurus

Asked to write an essay on modern sexuality and the role of androgyny in promiscuous social mores, your professor is less than impressed with your work entitled "Girls who are boys who like boys to be girls, who do boys like they're girls, who do girls like they're boys."

Pisces

You finally learn to appreciate rugby this week when somebody tells you to imagine that the pitch is Newcastle town centre three minutes before closing time and the ball is the last available bottle of vodka.

Gemini

Your business is firebombed for the third time this week. Maybe you shouldn't have called a dry cleaners that specialises in saris and turbans 'Ethnic Cleansing'?

Cancer

After your time working with Silvio Berlusconi, 'Extra virgin olive oil' sounds less like something you'd find in a food cupboard and more like a couple of orders for room service.

Aries

There are many unfashionable cuts of meat that are packed with flavour and can be picked up cheaply these days. Have some lung.

♌ Leo
Remember that the clocks go forward tonight. It'd be a shame to be late for all your Jeremy Kyle watching.

♍ Virgo
Everybody has their moment in the sun, and yours will come this week on page 12 under the headline "Ban This Pervert From Owning A Tortoise".

Libra
Your recent work to save the local library has been less about issues of child literacy and access to literature for the underprivileged and more about not wanting a load of pissy-smelling people hanging around the shopping arcade.

♏ Scorpio
Parting is such sweet sorrow that I shall say good night till it be morrow. I'm just going to stare at you while you're sleeping. Is that ok?

Sagittarius
Visiting your grandmother is a comforting reminder that for all the world's complicated hi-tech rush, there's still something to be said for a little old-fashioned wisdom. Just for god's sake don't mention gypsies.

Capricorn
I have often walked down this street before but the pavement always stayed beneath my feet before. All at once am I seven stories high, serves me right for strolling past a suspicious-looking car in Kabul during a riot.

Aquarius

You're not entirely convinced that your bosses are taking the issue of workplace sexism seriously this week when an email to HR generates the automated reply "Don't you worry your pretty little head about it, sweetcheeks".

Pisces

An unexpected visit from Satan this week as he points to page 43 of the new iTunes Terms & Conditions where you agreed to be his slave.

Aries

You suspect your neighbour's involvement when checking your street on Google Earth, you notice that somebody has written 'Gobshite' on the roof of your house.

Taurus

As a staunch opponent of multiculturalism, you firmly believe that troublemaking minority groups should be asked to leave the country for the good of everybody else. So as a privately-educated, Oxbridge graduate Tory MP, I expect you'll be leaving shortly?

Gemini

Everybody has started noticing the crow's feet around your eyes. Why don't you just buy normal glasses like everybody else?

Cancer

You break new ground in loneliness this week when that son of a diplomat in Nigeria with $20M waiting in a bank account asks you to stop emailing him.

Leo
Time to take the 3D television
back to the shops after watching
too much splay-legged Jamie
Redknapp punditry on Sky
Sports starts causing nightmares
that a pair of shiny grey
spacehoppers are trying to
attack you.

Scorpio
You're always wary of
pickpockets when you go
abroad because it would be
terrible if you couldn't stump
up bail money after drunkenly
beating up a load of foreigners
for walking about the place
being all foreign.

Virgo
No, I don't think strippers do
accept Nectar points, since
you ask.

Sagittarius
Like many before you, you turn
to drugs for artistic inspiration
and have to explain why your
latest single is a cover version
of *Night Nurse*.

Libra
Ever the victim of
misunderstandings, this week
you're kicked out of HMV for
asking the voluptuous shop
assistant whether she had
Smashing Pumpkins. Rubbing
your crotch and winking
probably didn't help.

Capricorn
It's generally accepted that
there's a direct correlation
between the length of your
coffee order and how much
of an unbearable tool you are.
How is your half-decaff skinny
Mocha with a shot of caramel?

Aquarius

One way of overcoming your fear of flying is to hijack a plane and crash-land it into the sea, proving that no matter what happens you'll still be safe. Or, y'know, hypnotherapy might work.

Taurus

Given your sedentary lifestyle and the history of heart disease in your family, you'll doubtless be surprised to hear that you're going to die at the age of 94 after a lorry full of dildos crashes into the nursing home.

Pisces

I want to make sure that this horoscope doesn't insult your intelligence but first I face the more difficult task of working out how such a thing could be possible.

Gemini

A visit from your sister is always a pleasure as you've often wondered what you'd have looked like if you'd given up your career at the age of 19 to eat pies.

Aries

This week I'd like you to beat somebody to death for having sex the wrong way. If anyone asks, tell them some bloke said it was wrong a couple of thousand years ago.

Cancer

Until somebody invents a virtual person for you to repeatedly elbow out of the way, as a pensioner online shopping is never going to be quite the same.

Leo

Medical opinion is divided on whether talking to people in comas is of any benefit to the patient, but most would agree you shouldn't be asking them if they mind you having all their stuff once they're gone.

Virgo

Sure, you could spend that last bit of money fending off your various creditors, or you could blow the lot on tasty cocktails with bits of fruit in them. What are they going to do, repossess your vomit?

Libra

As well as being a magnanimous loser it's also important to be graceful in victory, but I shouldn't worry too much about that second one any time soon.

Scorpio

While I appreciate it's a competitive job market at the moment, given that you're currently unemployed I'm not sure stuffing a tenner into each CV you send out is such a good idea.

Sagittarius

Fooling your inexplicably-hot wife that you're a computer salesman rather than a spy is just about on this side of implausible, but why has nobody in the secret service asked why they seem to have employed an Austrian bloke on steroids?

Scorpio

Dried goji berries are well-known for their antioxidant properties, so they should cancel out the coke you've cut them into, right?

"

Take time out to celebrate life's little victories, but going on a three-day bender after getting a parking space near the entrance of Tesco might be going a bit far.

"

Virgo

Famous Virgin:
Billy Ray Cyrus

Health:
You're a 20-a-day man, whether we're talking about cigarettes, pints of lager or sudden stabbing sensations down your left-hand side.

Career:
You'd love to tell your careers officer how wrong they were when they wrote you off as a teenager. Why not let them know the next time you're mopping the corridor outside their office?

Romance:
Love and marriage do indeed go together like a horse and carriage, as anybody who's canvassed the views of the horse on the whole arrangement will agree.

Highlight Of The Year:
Getting all the spaces stamped on your STD clinic loyalty card and receiving a free HIV test on the house.

Your Lucky One-Hit Wonder:
Stutter Rap - Morris Minor & The Majors

Aquarius

Clinging to the wheel arch of an articulated lorry with your few meagre possessions strapped to your back, you finally arrive in London to start making a better life for your family back home. You are aware there's a regular train service from Warrington, right?

Pisces

With the release of kebab-flavoured schnapps, your 40 years on the planet finally begin to make sense.

Aries

You always like to theme your parties and this weekend's appears to be along the lines of the Marie Celeste.

Taurus

It's important in life to know where you've come from and where you want to go to, because the slightest hesitation in your alibi will make the police suspicious.

Gemini

A spectacularly allergic reaction to shellfish this week as you break out into boils while watching an episode of *Spongebob Squarepants*.

Cancer

Excellent news this week as your long-standing issues with food, self-esteem and depression are all going to be sorted out by Davina McCall sneering at you and waving a Crème Egg under your nose.

Leo

Venison is not only a more intense flavour than beef, it has the added advantage of making kids cry when you tell them they're eating Bambi.

Virgo

I got a feeling, that tonight's gonna be a good night. That tonight's gonna be a good night. That tonight's gonna be a good night. Despite the fact that I'm in a Wetherspoons in Hartlepool pointing to the contrary.

Libra

An interesting eight seconds later this week as the last few moments of your life are spent realising that your entire journalistic career has been spent making an already dreadful world marginally worse with your pinch-mouthed hateful rambling. Enjoy hell.

Scorpio

As a general rule of thumb, I think it's usually a good idea to avoid taking pension planning advice from a man wearing a Viking helmet.

Sagittarius

Life's too short to hold on to regrets. Well, yours will be, anyway.

Capricorn

Encourage your kids to learn more about wildlife by leaving scraps of food by the back door and watch the wonder on their faces as they see their very first badger, fox or even a feral tramp.

Aquarius

There are many things that
make a person feel alive
– diving into a crystal ocean,
the first thrilling kiss of a love
affair – but right now I think
what the patient really needs is
50cc of adrenaline.

Taurus

You're proud to have brought
your daughters up with a
healthy attitude toward their
own body image, but with your
genetic timebomb of a fat arse,
that was the least you could do.

Pisces

The road is long, with many a
winding turn that leads us to
who knows where, who knows
where. Fucking TomTom.

Gemini

As an O2 customer, this week
you're offered priority booking
for UB40's latest tour in a
hitherto unheard-of usage of the
word 'priority'.

Aries

Don't rake up old grudges
at your forthcoming family
gathering. Make up a load
of new stuff to go absolutely
fucking mental about – it's what
your granddad would
have wanted.

Cancer

You've given your own spin on
the Spanish tradition of tapas
and a glass of salty Manzanilla
on the terrace by sitting in the
park with a bag of Tangy Toms
and a bottle of Harvey's
Bristol Cream.

Leo

Your lengthy, well-researched and biting critique into *Top Gear* is somewhat undermined by the fact that nobody with an ounce of common sense takes any notice of what Clarkson thinks and as a light entertainment program it means as much as a sparrow's fart in the grand scheme of things.

Virgo

You've managed to broaden your horizons after your recent city break to Bruges and can now add Belgians to the burgeoning list of people you have an irrational hatred of.

Libra

By the rivers of Babylon we sat and wept as we remembered Zion. Jesus, those *Matrix* sequels were rotten, weren't they?

Scorpio

Honesty is usually the best policy but owning a car in your part of town you may also wish to consider one that includes fire, theft and being driven through an off-license window.

Sagittarius

So you've turned 40. So what? Age is just a number, right? Well, so is 08457909090, for the Samaritans, and I'd rather you call them in future whenever you feel like having a whinge.

Capricorn

When it comes to picking long-running sitcoms, American ones will always win. Thus proving your old adage that "I can choose my 'Friends' but I can't choose 'My Family'."

Aquarius

Good for you this week for
sticking to your guns. Despite
the advice of friends, the
overwhelming evidence to
suggest you shouldn't and
prevailing European law. No,
really, well done you.

Pisces

After chatting with your boss
about the obscene bonuses
bankers get, he decides to
restructure everyone's wages
to reflect the value they add to
the company. Where you're
going to get your hands on the
£10,000 you now owe them is
anybody's guess.

Aries

Seeing as you've been
humming tunelessly at your
desk for the past four hours, I
was wondering whether you
knew the theme to *Casualty*?

Taurus

Between the 12th and 17th
week of your pregnancy the
baby will double in size, as
will the simmering sense of
resentment and anger over the
dinner table. Cherish these
moments.

Gemini

There's a fine line between
love and hate but there is an
enormous gulf between physical
attraction and what anybody of
the opposite sex is ever likely to
feel about you.

Cancer

You were worried the other day
when you had that agonising,
crushing sensation in your
chest, but fortunately you went
numb all down one arm so that
alleviated it a little.

Leo

Shot through the heart, and you're to blame, you give love a bad name. Not to mention archery tuition.

Virgo

Bosses at Yellow Pages are unhappy with your ad campaign pitch this week, featuring a 70 year-old man going to various smut shops asking if they have an old gay porn film starring Storm Assblaster. "My name....?"

Libra

It's your third month in the Magnet kitchen factory this week and it's only fair to warn you that if you make one more 'counter productive' joke you're going to get a sink unit across the throat.

Scorpio

Your employment tribunal finds that, despite your insistence, the second line of "One, two, buckle my shoe" is definitely not "Three, four, big fat whore".

Sagittarius

You're becoming increasingly worried that you may be beaten up for your iPhone, not because somebody may want to steal it, but because it marks you out as a tit.

Capricorn

Not the greatest start to your career at the British Film Institute when you put together a proposal for a Martin Short retrospective. Even the inclusion of *Father Of The Bride II* didn't swing it.

Aquarius

If you're worried that the lights keep intermittently cutting out in your flat, that's what's known as 'blinking'.

Pisces

If you're on the train, there's nothing stopping you sitting opposite a young woman. Or trying to shift a bit of food out of a rear molar. Or picking an egg stain off the front of your jeans. But doing all three simultaneously might incur the involvement of the transport police.

Aries

It's very exciting to hear your friends are having a baby, because given their collection of neuroses and varying levels of flakiness, there's no telling what the little fucker is going to turn out like.

Taurus

No, don't worry about it, mine humps people's legs, too. So, was yours born that way or were they dropped on their head?

Gemini

Your night classes studying art are really paying off – where you used to consider Banksy to be "shit", you're now able to more eloquently describe him as "absolute and utter fucking shit".

Cancer

Restless legs in bed are usually just a symptom of iron deficiency but I think in your case it may be your body's way of saying you've never had nearly enough late-night fun. 11pm on a Friday? Are you a quadraplegic nun or something?

Leo

The project you're heading has gone down in flames, is way over budget and is failing to meet any of its targets. Time to do the responsible thing as leader and decide whose fault it is.

Virgo

Exciting her with the power of the magic blue pill has never been easier! Your powerful manhandle will make her weep with joy! You will also come into conflict with a close friend over money this week.

Libra

You're quite right that Rome wasn't built in a day but I imagine that even whilst wearing a toga they managed to mow the fucking lawn once in a while.

Scorpio

After patiently explaining the way brand-name trainers are manufactured in third world sweatshops, your child promises to stop asking for them. On the condition you buy them a pair of elbow-length rubber gloves to retrieve the enormous wedgies they're going to be given for the rest of their school life.

Sagittarius

One love, one heart, let's get together and feel alright. Ah, the clarion call of lonely masturbators everywhere.

Capricorn

Your fiendish plan to avoid prosecution works as the defence lawyer reveals at the crucial moment that all of your testimony was given with your fingers crossed.

Aquarius
Your priorities change throughout your life – as a kid all you cared about were sweets, as you get old it will be having somewhere safe and secure to live – and right now your number one priority is finding enough ketamine to mindfuck a glacier before Friday night. Good for you.

Pisces
If you think you have the skills and mindset required to become a Royal Marine, for Christ's sake join the army or you'll end up in jail.

Aries
Buying a sofa has made you feel like a real grownup. Well, you had to buy it after you broke it playing 'trampoline'.

Taurus
This week you'll have a moment like that Hollywood cliché where the couple have a blazing row before tumbling into a passionate embrace, only replacing the passionate embrace with an acrimonious breakup that ultimately tears both of your lives apart.

Gemini
The correct scientific name for a fear of clowns is Coulrophobia, which comes from the Greek word for "Keep those freaky-faced, serial-killing fuckers away from me".

Cancer
So many costs involved in running a car – tax, insurance, MOT – and this week there's another £150 to fork out having the boot steam-cleaned before the police get a warrant.

Leo

It's always the highlight of your day working in a jeweller's when somebody returns an engagement ring and you get to the bit of the refund form that asks 'reason for refund request'.

Virgo

When most people fantasise about winning the lottery, they browse the internet for sports cars and expensive foreign holidays. You're currently having MSN conversations with a 'fixer' called Sergei who knows all there is to know about the properties of quicklime and removing fingerprints. You do love a grudge, don't you?

Libra

You can't have your cake and eat it. Not if you want to carry on working in Greggs, anyway.

Scorpio

Turning down your thermostat by just five degrees could save you £50 a year in fuel bills. But Roy down the pub, who's a whizz with a gas meter and an industrial hoover, could actually have Eon owing you money.

Sagittarius

You'll never forget when he proposed in that restaurant and they gave you free champagne. Because he now does it every time you go out to eat. And the staff in KFC are less than three months from working it out.

Capricorn

Eating olives, listening to Miles Davis and leafing through a volume of modern art, you realise that being an adult is a pile of shit. From now on it's Sugar Puffs, an X-Men comic and Madness on the stereo.

"

You've no real moral compass, charm, useful skills or compassion to offer the world but given that you're quite exceptionally good-looking it's never really come up in conversation.

"

Libra

Famous Librarian:
Winnie Mandela

Health:
Please consult your doctor before making any changes to your diet.
Although I'm pretty sure they'd be fine with you laying off the
meat pie and macaroni cheese sandwiches.

Career:
Just because you work in a fertility clinic doesn't mean you're the
only one who spends all day surrounded by tossers, you know.

Romance:
Since meeting your new partner, all those songs you used to hear
on the radio finally make sense. Especially the ones by Slipknot.

Highlight Of The Year:
Seeing those strange lights in the sky, waking up three days
later in a skip with a sore arse and having your faith in extra-
terrestrials renewed. Those Turkish sailors you met seemed
pleased with your story, too.

Your Lucky One-Hit Wonder:
Just Say No – The Cast of Grange Hill

Aquarius

The power of love is a curious thing. Makes one man weep, makes another man sing. Or, in your case, erect a shrine in your spare room featuring hundreds of photographs with the eyes cut out.

Taurus

I don't think constantly washing your hands counts as OCD if you're a surgeon, really. Collecting bottles of your own piss and filing them in date order is a different matter, though.

Pisces

Your new camera is absolutely brilliant and takes pictures so sharp you can actually see the look of panic, revulsion and forced bonhomie in the eyes of your friends as they pose with you. Do you want your old one back?

Gemini

Context is everything, as you learn this week. Laughing at a kid that's been shoved off a swing on *You've Been Framed* is fine, but shoving one off the swing in the park and laughing loudly into their sobbing face is apparently "not on".

Aries

Smearing shit on somebody's window is a classic form of revenge but one piece of advice I'd give is to not try doing it when they're going 40mph.

Cancer

Everybody is jealous of your life as part of the pit crew for a Formula 1 team, little realising that it's basically like working in Kwik-Fit for petulant arseholes whilst battling jet-lag.

Leo

Your cynicism has plumbed such depths that you're doubtless reading this with a weary sigh and waiting for the insult at the end. And I'd hate to disappoint you, you dreary arsehole.

Virgo

Remember when you were a teenager and you said you'd rather die than live to the age of 40? Happy 39th, you wrinkly failure.

Libra

He was something generally feckless and essentially juvenile. She was something fairly uptight and obsessed with order. But when they got together, it was 90 minutes of crushingly-obvious chalk & cheese cockwiffle.

Scorpio

Making your own gnocchi is surprisingly straightforward and so much better than shop-bought. There is the potential for becoming an unbelievably self-satisfied prick but I think we passed that several Youtube clips of your kid's clarinet recitals ago.

Sagittarius

You've always used homeopathy and other alternative medicines to treat your ailments and who's to say you're wrong? Me. I am. You're wrong.

Capricorn

You're always the model of courtesy as you wave drivers out of a side street onto a busy main road. They probably wouldn't look so terrified if you were sat in a car.

Aquarius

You've always felt that rugby union is a much more manly game than football, but that's mostly because you associate manliness with public school education, shared baths and an obsession with your teammates' genitals.

Taurus

A stark realisation this week as you find that using previous sexual encounters as masturbatory fantasies becomes less an exercise in imagination and more an exercise in memory retention. Still, cheaper than a Nintendo DS.

Pisces

Telling your Facebook friends you've just had a very interesting meeting will make them think you're being headhunted or making a film or something. They don't need to know it was with your blackmailer.

Gemini

After a quest taking 30 years, spanning six continents and costing your home, your friends and your sanity, you finally locate the fabled fountain of youth. And wouldn't you know it, it's now a fucking Starbucks.

Aries

Expect a visit from the police after your application to be on the show *Embarrassing Bodies* includes a photo of your secret freezers.

Cancer

Some people can't take a joke, such as your girlfriend when you grab a handful of her stretch marks and ask whether her real surname is Armstrong.

Leo

Raise a glass of champagne for a very special occasion this week – it's been five years since you overcame the crippling alcoholism that nearly cost you everything!

Virgo

A mixed reception for your US version of *The Hairy Bikers Cookbook*, which mostly takes place in a methamphetamine lab and has a considerably higher amount of pool cues and racist beatings than its UK counterpart.

Libra

It's perfectly possible to feed a young family with fresh, healthy produce for less money than it would cost to buy processed food. But as you've correctly identified, they are only kids after all, so fuck them.

Scorpio

It's not unusual to be loved by anyone, it's not unusual to have fun with anyone, but it is quite unusual to ask them to dress up like Des Lynam while you're doing it.

Sagittarius

You must be very proud of the fact that you're multilingual, can play several instruments and have written that novel you were always talking about. Or you would be if you'd ever got off your spotty arse to do any of those things. Still, you've completed every *GTA* game ever released so that's something.

Capricorn

If you're happy and you know it clap your hands. Anything to keep them away from your crotch for five minutes.

Aquarius

I think the main reason you recently failed your history exam was stating that one of the major problems caused by the hyperinflation of Germany in the 1920s was that it made filming *The Price Is Right* essentially impossible.

Taurus

The sight of you sat alone, blowing out the birthday candle you've stuck in your apple pie, has managed to top the list of the most tragic things the staff of McDonalds have ever seen. Bravo!

Pisces

If you're going through financial difficulties, emotional problems or health fears, don't suffer in silence. Go absolutely bastard mental and start screaming about them at a busy dual carriageway intersection.

Gemini

You often feel you're being too puerile and childish but it's obvious you're being too hard on yourself. All you need to... oh, wait a minute, did I just say 'hard on'? Brilliant!

Aries

A surprise visit at 3am this week from a television producer who gives you ideas of new ways you can wait tables. Just to see how you fucking well like it.

Cancer

As the global recession finally bites Hollywood, you're disappointed by your recent visit to the cinema after the latest *Bourne Identity* appears to be that of a middle-aged chartered surveyor.

Leo

This is the modern world and most people have probably checked their emails or Facebook during a visit to the loo. But an eight-man *World Of Warcraft* raiding party is going to give you piles.

Virgo

If you're worried that women will notice that you have the conversational skills of a concrete mixer, simply do half a billion press-ups so your upper body looks like you're stood in front of a convex window. They love that.

Libra

You're well-known in your family for your gag gifts, and grandma's this year is a cracker. It's made of leather and has studs and everything.

Scorpio

Pisces, Pluto and Mars combine this week when you go on holiday to Norway and end up accidentally eating a chocolate bar that's been licked by a dog.

Scorpio

Your court case against Snappy Snaps is unlikely to go anywhere, given that the main body of your complaint is that the beach photos make you look like 12 stone of uncooked sausage meat.

Sagittarius

Following the tradition of breaking a bottle of champagne to christen the maiden voyage of a ship, this week you write off a 10-year-old Citreon Saxo with a can of Stella.

Aquarius

As you approach middle age, the one thing you're not worried about is the state of your prostate gland as all the years of wanking have meant that even now it's so strong you could piss shut a fire door.

Pisces

BBC2 aren't going for your new cocktail show idea, where celebrities flick a matchstick over their shoulder at a bar four times and drink whatever that ends up creating. Not even after you show them the self-filmed pilot of Dean Gaffney getting proper fucked up.

Aries

I'm in the mood for love, simply because you're near me, although if I'm being honest the three Es are helping immensely.

Taurus

Good for you for campaigning in your local election. It must be exhausting having to use the phrase "insidious influence of the Jew" 400 times a day.

Gemini

While purchasing yourself a Kindle to encourage you to read more books would generally be commended by others, if you're going to fill it up with John Grisham and Harry Potter, you may as well have bought yourself a bag of chocolate-covered arse winnets.

Cancer

Grief comes in five distinct stages, six if you include the stage where your bored friends tell you to shut the fuck up and get over it.

Leo

Men often say that the hardest thing about having an affair is having to keep up the constant deceit but it's actually the bit where you try and find another human being prepared to have sex with you.

Virgo

Whenever you feel alone, remember that your grandparents are looking down from above, willing you on and possibly wishing that you'd unlock the hatch in the attic now and again.

Libra

If you're struggling to decide where to go on holiday this year, why not eat a semi-defrosted fish finger so you vomit for a fortnight, press your face into a griddle pan and stay at home?

Scorpio

You've managed to ride out the recession thus far by using the simple expedient of having bugger-all money to begin with.

Sagittarius

Make a romantic gesture by taking your partner on a horse-drawn carriage ride around the park, because nothing says 'I love you' like an hour of hypothermia staring at an 18-inch anus and sniffing semi-digested hay.

Capricorn

Anyone accusing you of lazy racism might want to try and spend 12 hours a day thinking of ways to make Jeremy Clarkson appear funny. Not to mention writing a script for Hammond that doesn't make his brain go all wonky.

Aquarius

Yes, I'm getting hints of burnt paper, vinegary overtones and a suggestion of tin. I do love eating sandwiches I've found in the bin.

Pisces

Your meal is about to reach tipping point in the restaurant as you've sent it back so many times that it's now more semen than food.

Aries

This weekend, why not stage a real-life version of Pacman by wandering around a branch of DFS avoiding the salesmen 'ghosts'? But when they eventually corner you and ask if you need any help, you have to make the proper "Weeoow-eeooweeoowackwack" death noise.

Taurus

First of all you spoil the silence of the quiet train carriage by gitting into your mobile phone about tit-all and now by screaming at me to stop hitting you. Can't you just shut up?

Gemini

After noticing that aliens seem to spend most of their time mucking around with crops, doing unspeakable things to cattle and forcibly probing men's bottoms, you've come to the inescapable conclusion that we're being visited by inter-galactic Welshmen.

Cancer

Relax. Things cannot be as bad as you think they are. Now, just calmly tell me what the problem is. Right. Okay. Uh-huh. Nope, I was wrong, you're screwed.

Leo

Selling Avon products has opened up whole new avenues for you recently. Now you can just knock on somebody's front door and bore them unannounced.

Scorpio

It's not been easy for you to get in the Christmas spirit this year, given that you're skint, Sikh and a miserable bastard. Are you sure you should be running the Grotto, then?

Virgo

Your favourite sitcom is *Two And A Half Men*, your favourite Beatle is Ringo and your favourite wine gums are the green ones. No, seriously though, what the hell is wrong with you?

Sagittarius

You've written an imaginative reinvention of the Dickens classic, but is the world ready for a Scrooge that fires Bob Cratchett on Christmas Day because he's had a bad night's sleep?

Libra

You've been using the mental image of Margaret Thatcher having her first dump of the day as an ejaculation retardant for so long that you're now unable to maintain an erection without it.

Capricorn

Good King Wenceslas looked out, on the feast of Stephen, as the snow lay round about, deep and crisp and even. So he tossed another pauper onto the fire and closed the curtains.

> **"**
> *You've always viewed your sexuality as a fluid entity, veering between homosexual, heterosexual and when the mood takes you, architectural.*
> **"**

Scorpio

Famous Scorpuscle: Judy Finnegan

Health:
As the most sexually-active of all the star signs, you're also the most likely to visit your local A&E department with a tiny mammal in your rectum and to ask them for 'the usual'.

Career:
You're sick of looking at your payslip and seeing most of your wages disappear in deductions - National Insurance, Income Tax, pension, hush money to the Albanian mafia...

Romance:
Don't feel insecure just because your other half is younger, better-looking, cleverer and more charming than you are. You've got something special that will keep you together forever.
The key to the cellar.

Highlight Of The Year:
Standing behind the local newsreader during a live broadcast and making it look like she's got antlers as she covers the story of that orphanage burning down.

Your Lucky One-Hit Wonder:
Mouldy Old Dough - Lieutenant Pigeon

Aquarius

For those about to rock, we
salute you. For those about
to Coldplay, we hope you get
Lupus.

Pisces

It takes two to tango, but
it takes at least five for an
officially recognised
daisy chain.

Aries

Your rollover Euro lottery win
this week gives you the chance
to pose the organisers of Comic
Relief a moral quandary as
you offer to donate £20m if 30
minutes of the show consists
of James Corden encased in
concrete apart from his head
and then lowered upside down
into a vat of your shit.

Taurus

For future reference, if you're
at a dinner party and somebody
remarks that the rise of the
Nazis was a lesson we must
never forget, it's best not to
remark "Yes, the lesson being
that they were sloppy".

Gemini

As it's your 20th wedding
anniversary this week,
really push the boat out for
your celebration meal. By
Supersizing it.

Cancer

An exciting week as you're
called for a TV commercial
casting, giving you the
opportunity to beg for the
chance to whore your so-called
art for a little bag of pennies.

Leo

Fuck tha police! Fuck, fuck, fuck tha police! Fuck tha police! Fuck, fuck, fuck tha police! Ooooh, that's better.

Virgo

You must change what you cannot accept, accept what you cannot change and have the wisdom to not phone me at 1am to whinge about it you unconscionable fucknut.

Libra

Your interview for the LGBT police liason officer takes a downward turn when you ask whether the role would involve bumming.

Scorpio

You return from your Jamaican holiday full of beans and, thanks to that guy you met on the beach, bunged up with heroin-filled johnny bags.

Sagittarius

It's never too late to say you're sorry, even if it means screaming it through the coffin lid while a clutch of sobbing relatives desperately try dragging you away.

Capricorn

When you die, people are going to say you've had a good innings. Unfortunately, given that they're all English, that's going to mean about 28.

Aquarius

Most people can't relate their own experience of losing their virginity to scenes in Hollywood movies, but you can, thanks to that laundry room scene in *The Shawshank Redemption*.

Pisces

I don't think it can be called 'burlesque' if you pass a pint glass around the pub so you'll blow somebody on stage.

Aries

You manage to impress the staff at the classical music counter of HMV when you ask for "That one that's on when Susan Sarandon is lezzing up in that vampire film".

Taurus

Here's a horoscope I prepared earlier - money worries, with a slight touch of herpes.

Gemini

A terrible dilemma this week as you're halfway through having a haircut and a Stereophonics song comes on the radio. A half-shaved head or sitting through *Mr Writer*? Tough call.

Cancer

Your friends and family are going to be absolutely shocked when you die and it comes to light that you've been wearing a wig all these years because it's a remarkably lifelike piece of work. There must be some other reason people nudge each other and giggle whenever you walk past.

Leo

There's no nicer way of working off a sumptuous meal at a fabulous restaurant than running like greased fuck down the street whilst being chased by a gang of irate waiters.

Scorpio

If people don't take your opinion on cinema seriously, it may be because your top ten favourite film list includes the words "XI" and "Assploitation".

Virgo

Only by facing your fears can you overcome them. Unfortunately your fear is faces.

Sagittarius

Error #51082 - star sign not recognised. Please re-enter date of birth.

Libra

Remember there are many alternative painkilling solutions on the market that don't rely on chemicals, analgesics and science. And without exception they're all absolutely fucking useless.

Capricorn

The bottle stated it was a subtle infusion of 42 herbs from a recipe used by monks since the 17th century so you think they'd have space on the label to mention that three litres of it would make you feel like you'd tried to headbutt a comet.

Aquarius

Treat yourself to one piece of chocolate a day during your diet for all your hard work. Of course an entire bar counts as one piece, you absolute superhero.

Taurus

Playing classical music to your baby in the womb has been known to boost its IQ, so I reckon with a looped tape of Bach you're good for about 20 fags a day to balance it out.

Pisces

This week, in a strange case of life imitating art, everyone you meet will be balding with curly hair and singing *Bridge Over Troubled Water*.

Gemini

If the name everybody uses to refer to you ends in "-meister" and you're not a German mayor then it means you must be a tit.

Cancer

When your eyes meet across a crowded bar, a nod, a wink and a wiggle of the eyebrows is all you need to do to let her know you've got chronic Tourettes.

Aries

It's not unusual for a doctor to ask for a stool sample but it is generally considered bad form if they do it on a first date.

Leo

That ring in your nose does
make you look really rock 'n'
roll. Specifically Black Sabbath.
More specifically *War Pigs*.

Virgo

It's very easy to sit at home
criticising the likes of Peter Kay
and Michael McIntyre, calling
their comedy cliched and lazy
and bemoaning a general public
that bovinely eats the whole
unappetising mess up.
So crack on.

Libra

What with judgement day
coming up and the four
horsemen of the apocalypse
roaming the land, now may not
be the best time to start making
gay porn to pay for your
crack habit.

Scorpio

After the success of post-work
restaurants Thank God It's
Friday's you launch a chain of
depressing drinking holes called
Fuck You Satan, It's Monday.

Sagittarius

Not satisfied with the dozens of
products you've bought to wage
war on every single microbe
that might be in your home,
giving your toddler leukemia,
you develop your own 60,000
gallon portable bath to disinfect
your entire house. You are
going to make a mint.

Capricorn

While leaving your body to
the local medical school is a
laudable gesture, in your case
it's actually rather unfair. Even
to students.

Aquarius

Russell Brand is a monumental cunt. Sorry for hijacking your horoscope but it needed saying.

Pisces

Fear of the unknown is most people's biggest fear. Yours should be the fact you never got around to having the electrics checked in your new home.

Aries

If you're writing a script set in the past, always throw in a bit of dialogue that the audience knows will turn out to be untrue - "I see that Hitler chap's getting a bit shirty over in Germany. None of our concern, though." - because that never sounds clunky or shit.

Taurus

My milkshake brings all the boys to the yard. So much so that the Commissioner has asked me to stop bringing it in to work.

Gemini

You'll never forget where you were on the day the repressive dictatorship of your home country was toppled and the people took their first sweet breaths as free men and women. You were setting fire to a shitload of incriminating documents and legging it out of the parliament building with a suitcase full of stolen art.

Cancer

The best thing to counteract the effects of chilli is yoghurt rather than water. An absolute bastard to get onto your beef hula hoop, though.

Leo

Getting older isn't all bad
– you've now reached the
age where sitting on the train
with your fly gaping open
is considered more a sign of
harmless absentmindedness
and less an extraordinarily bold
sexual gambit.

Virgo

You were working as a waitress
in a cocktail bar when I met
you. That was 40 minutes ago.
So I have to ask – where the
fuck is my Mojito?

Libra

You finally crack the secret of
eternal sexual bliss by turning
the humble circle jerk into the
Möbius Strip jerk.

Scorpio

Either your elderly neighbour
has bought a Harley Davidson
and has taken to revving it all
hours of the day and night or
it's time they stopped trying to
digest eggs.

Sagittarius

'Wino' is such a pejorative term
and 'street drinker' too clinical,
which is why you prefer to be
known as 'The Human Drip
Tray'. Sounds more
superhero-y.

Capricorn

Things turn out better than
expected this week as your four-
day standoff with the police
ends not in a hail of bullets but
in a light drizzle of a fucking
good kicking.

Aquarius

A long, hearty laugh can be
as beneficial to your health as
a workout in the gym so why
not save membership money
by shoving a pensioner into the
road twice a week?

Pisces

You've reached the point in
your life when the endless cycle
of ketamine, whoremongering
and seedy bars has become
boring. And besides, the
Archbishop's going to find out
sooner or later.

Aries

The ability to empathise with
the suffering of your fellow
man and perform acts of
truly selfless altruism is what
separates us from our primate
ancestors. Fancy a banana?

Taurus

Your mind is a constant,
giddying whir of schemes,
ideas, inventions and plots.
Each one of them infinitely
shitter than the last.

Gemini

Your boss always has a hidden
agenda, which makes taking the
minutes to meetings a fucking
headache if nothing else.

Cancer

That awful nightmare where
you snap and start sobbing
questions into the terrified
faces of your fellow commuters
finally comes true this week,
but don't worry. It gets replaced
with a new dream that's way
more disturbing.

Leo

People accuse you of being obsessed with sex and that's true, but only in the same sense drowning people are 'obsessed' with oxygen.

Virgo

Your creative meeting with Christian Bale doesn't go well this week after you suggest he open the next film running toward the screen singing "Bat-maaaan! Dinnaninnanin-naninna-Batmaaaan!"

Libra

You may find it easier to make friends if you stopped insisting on addressing everybody as 'unworthy scum' and shoehorning your plans for global annihilation into every conversation.

Scorpio

All the planets and most of the stars align this week in a straight line that points directly to under your bed. Time to come clean about what's there.

Sagittarius

Your healer indicates that your aura has turned from a pleasant, rosy pink to a more unsettling shade of green this week and fuck my tired old face if it's not going to cost 300 sheets for him to sort it out. Couldn't you just roll around in a load of paint instead?

Capricorn

It's an exciting time for you right now as the demands of your solipsism, blank-eyed cruelty and boundless competitiveness all compete to take control of the nativity play you're directing.

> *In several trillion years time, the last ebb of energy from the last atom in the universe will weakly pulse for the final time and history itself will cease to exist. So failing to give a modicum of a shit about your problems is, in a cosmic sense, eminently sensible. Actually, just shut the fuck up.*

Sagittarius

Famous Sagitator:
Fiddy Cent

Health:
The nagging pain in your shoulder that's been troubling you for years is going to be replaced by a searing white-hot agony that makes you feel like you're wearing a molten steel handbag. Progress, of a sort.

Career:
Your chronic philandering finally synchronises into something beneficial this year as you manage to claim for four sets of paternity leave one after another, meaning you don't spend a single day in work.

Romance:
Lovers may come and go but you'll always have your friends. Until you have sex with them and drive them away with your freaky demands, too.

Highlight Of The Year:
The ascending of your previously-pendulous hemorrhoids.

Your Lucky One-Hit Wonder:
Rock Me Amadeus - Falco

Aquarius

Are you still alive?
What an oversight.

Pisces

You've reached the stage in
your relationship where you
can break wind in front of
each other. But getting the
dictaphone out when you think
that "This one's a keeper" might
be a sign the magic's gone.

Aries

Who ya gonna call?
Ghostbusters? To treat your anal
polyps? Seriously?

Taurus

Your boss is amazed that
your 10-minute lunch breaks
have actually doubled your
productivity in the afternoons,
probably because he's never
done chunky fat lines of
banker's chalk in a stationery
cupboard.

Gemini

This week somebody mentions
the Catholic church and you
kick yourself for not being the
first amongst your friends to
mention child abuse in a lazy
attempt to use the suffering of
thousands to appear edgy.

Cancer

And when you get that feeling,
you want sexual healing. 'That
feeling' being a persistent itch
and a burning sensation when
you piss.

Leo

Good job your house was built near some caves and not a giant flower garden, otherwise Gotham City would currently be protected by a man dressed as an enormous bee.

Scorpio

A recent survey found the most commonly-used phrase in the movies these days is "let's get the hell outta here".
Are there really that many Jude Law films?

Virgo

After 30 years climbing up the dangerous ladder of the criminal underworld, you ask yourself why you still need to have meetings in a dingy nightclub with a bored stripper in the background. How much can office space cost these days?

Sagittarius

Your two biggest fears are that nobody else has the same dark wishes screaming around the haunted caverns of their skull and that everyone else is going to find out that you do. Well, I've got some bad news and some really, really bad news.

Libra

If $(z1-y) + 3x = .25a$, where (a) is a positive integer, then you're fucked into a cocked hat.

Capricorn

This week, your ideal partner will come into your life. Riding on a unicorn that can cure cancer. Yeah, right.

Aquarius

Rah rah, ah ah ah. Roma, roma ma. Gaga ooh la la. I think that covers all the main points.

Pisces

As somebody who habitually spends their time sat in a bath full of baked beans while dressed as the Pope, you hate Comic Relief as much as any sane person would.

Aries

As a retired footballer you envy the younger lads being busy week in, week out but every now and then you still manage to bang an anonymous model in a Travelodge.

Taurus

Nobody likes doing housework but your habit of sealing up the flat with concrete and selling it every time the bins need emptying is proving costly.

Gemini

Two cups of espresso in the morning really jolts you awake and keeps you regular, especially because you have them as an enema.

Cancer

'Race For Life'? Five kilometres? And you want sponsoring for that? Are you actually fucking kidding me? Tell you what, how about I sponsor you £10 for every load of washing you put in the fucking machine? What? Missing what point, exactly?

♌ Leo
Remember the old adage "Dance like nobody's watching and sing like nobody's listening" because believe me, absolutely nobody is.

♏ Scorpio
Ever since you were at school you've been told to pull your socks up, not because you're lazy but because your knees look like a haggis made of knuckles.

♍ Virgo
My my, at Waterloo Napoleon did surrender. Oh yeah, and I have met my destiny in quite a similar way. Not that I'm trying to compare the decisive battle for the fate of 19th-century Europe with getting my fanny seen to, obviously.

Sagittarius
If you really didn't want your daughter growing up to be a stripper, was giving her a double-barrelled forename - where one of them had a 'y' where an 'i' should be - a good idea?

Libra
As you patiently explain to the person in HR during your disciplinary hearing, you cannot possibly be a racist as you used to love Rusty Lee when she was on the telly.

Capricorn
Llanfairpwllgwyngyllgo-gerychwyrndrobwllllantysi-liogogogoch. Or 'The noise a Welshman makes when retrieving his frisbee from an electricity pylon', as you discover this week.

Aquarius
Smoking a pipe does give you a certain air of gravitas, but leave off during cunnilingus, there's a good chap.

Pisces
Your new wet/dry hoover keeps your carpet amazingly clean but you know what else would work? Not being such a cackhanded moron and occasionally treating your dog's worms.

Aries
You're beginning to regret booking such a cheap holiday this week after a long session by the pool reveals that your partner has been writing the word 'cock' on your forehead with SPF50 while you've been asleep.

Taurus
Your new haircut couldn't make you look any more of a cunt if they'd grafted a clitoris onto your forehead.

Gemini
She came from Greece, she had a thirst for knowledge. She studied sculpture at St. Martin's College, that's where I caught her eye. So now I'm only allowed to do it over her boobs.

Cancer
If this were a Hollywood movie, the accusations of assault, terrorism and sexual harassment would just be part of a government conspiracy to bring you down because you know too much. But we've both seen the piles of Kestrel Super empties, the blackouts and the sobbing visits to the laundrette, so we both know that's not true.

♌ Leo

Learned men throughout the ages have wrestled with truth, beauty, morality and even the very nature of existence itself without finding an answer. But go on, we're on our sixth pint, so tell me what your philosophy on life is. Eight pence says it has something to do with living each day like it's your last.

♍ Virgo

You're right, having the letter you had printed in the local newspaper blown up to six-foot square, laminated and hung over the fireplace does make a striking centrepiece. You big psychopath.

Libra

Uh-huh. Yeah. Right. Mmmm-hmmm. Okay. Yep. What? No, of course I wasn't fucking listening.

♏ Scorpio

While complaining to customer services in Waitrose about the freshness of the Coquille St Jacques this week you catch sight of yourself in the mirror behind them, have a blinding moment of self-awareness, and start crying.

Sagittarius

Being a panelist on a topical news show is a lot more difficult than it looks as it can take literally an hour to shoehorn bits of the set you've been performing for the last five years into the script.

Capricorn

Life is merely the prelude to the main feature that is the afterlife. That's why yours seems so disjointed, dull and full of adverts.

Aquarius

Everybody's had a difficult year and nobody is really in a position to buy pricey gifts for friends, but sending everybody an invoice for the drinks you've bought them over the last 12 months is possibly going a bit far.

Taurus

Your plan to use those retro 70s crackers you found in the loft backfires spectacularly as your daughter's new boyfriend reads the joke that starts "How many darkies does it take to change a lightbulb?"

Pisces

Turkey can be horribly dry if it's overcooked and obviously you want to avoid giving your guests food poisoning by undercooking it. So when they come around, just nod your head at the kitchen and tell them to do it their sodding selves.

Gemini

Invent a new drinking game this Christmas by downing a pint of Advocaat during the Queen's speech every time she mentions the Commonwealth.

Cancer

The living room floor is littered with wrapping paper everywhere. Not the most imaginative present to buy everyone but they'll be glad of it come next December.

Aries

New year, new you. Right, how about one with slightly less ear hair?

Leo

MMMMMEEEE
RRRRYYYYYY CHRRR
RRIIIIIIIoh I can't be fucking
bothered.

Virgo

The kids were so excited
when they heard the sound of
footsteps and sleighbells on
the roof last night so there's
no point in spoiling things by
telling them you were chasing
off that paedophile morris
dancer from down the road.

Libra

Try to make your resolutions
a bit more realistic this year.
Nothing with the words
'marathon' or 'Everest' or
a proposed reduction in
wonderfully cheap
Ukrainian wine.

Scorpio

New Year's Day traditionally
heralds the worst hangover
you're going to experience all
year, so your level of optimism
should progressively increase
throughout the months. Never
really works out that way
though, does it?

Sagittarius

Well done for quitting smoking
and facing up to a life without
the sweet lung caress of that
irresistible whore nicotine and
f...oh go on, light one up for
me, too.

Capricorn

With your bad back getting
increasingly worse, the price
of gaffer tape going through
the roof and the number of
hitchhikers dwindling, it's not
going to be a great sacrifice
giving up your main vice.

Aquarius

12 months without being thrown off a bus with your unsheathed cock fountaining piss everywhere. Is that too much to ask?

Pisces

Yes, it probably is offensive to a billion people to refer to Chinese New Year as 'Resolution Do-Over Day', actually.

Aries

Well, that's Christmas and New Year over with, the next big celebration is going to be Valentine's D...oh would you please stop crying?

Taurus

Hey, this New Year is going to be completely different and is guaranteed to be the point at which things start looking up. Yes, I am automatically assuming your life's been shit recently. I just play the percentage.

Gemini

You're starting the year as you mean to go on – bilious, drunk and surrounded by chocolate and tinsel. High-five, big man.

Cancer

Today is the first day of the rest of your life, raising the horrifying prospect of going through puberty all over again.

Leo

Colleagues have been complimenting your boss on her new bracelet all day, so well done for suggesting it must chafe horribly while she's wanking off strangers in the bus station bogs.

Scorpio

An epiphany this week as you realise your ability to read off a handout and order tea and coffee means you're more than qualified to earn £800 a day delivering corporate training.

Virgo

Before considering mass redundancies, your company is going to have a period of consultation, in much the same way a lion consults a gazelle on the subject of lunch.

Sagittarius

You've got your sneaky internet porn habit so finely trained now that you can throw yourself about to some grot and get yourself wiped down in the time it takes the missus to put the bins out.

Libra

Heads and shoulders knees and toes, knees and toes. I'm telling you, never buy a fridge off Denis Nilsen.

Capricorn

By entering the data on the position of the stars for every second over the last 20 years, I've managed to map out precisely what your fate is going to be. It starts with me asking you why I fucking bothered.

Capricorn

Famous Capricornucopean: Carol Smillie

Health:
If you continue suffering from sluggish reactions, coldness in the extremities, lack of appetite and reduced heart rate, you may have to face up to the fact that you're actually dead.

Career:
You're beginning to regret installing that suggestion box as this is the third time this month you've had to call the fire brigade to help somebody remove their dick from it.

Romance:
Love is patient, love is kind. It does not envy, it does not boast, it is not proud. It does not dishonour others, it is not self-seeking, it is not easily angered, it keeps no record of wrongs. So stop fucking banging on about the washing up.

Highlight Of The Year:
Sitting on the ledge atop the multi-storey carpark as the indifferent throb of humanity rush past below and realising that in about eight seconds you're not going to have to worry about it any longer. Silver lining and all that.

Your Lucky One-Hit Wonder: Who Let The Dogs Out? - Baha Men